JEWISH
NEW YORK

~~Dear you~~ Kent,

Enjoy your journey through Jewish New York! I look forward to working with you.

Paul Kaplan

www.paulkaplanauthor.com

Henry Street Settlement, one of New York's most historic and important social-service agencies, was established by Lillian D. Wald. At its inception in 1893, the settlement served primarily Jewish, Italian, and Irish immigrants. Today, it still serves immigrants, many of them of Chinese and Latino descent. (Photograph courtesy Jessica Siemens)

JEWISH
NEW YORK
A History and Guide
to Neighborhoods,
Synagogues, and Eateries

Paul M. Kaplan

PELICAN PUBLISHING COMPANY
Gretna 2015

The word "Pelican" and the depiction of a pelican are
trademarks of Pelican Publishing Company, Inc., and are
registered in the U.S. Patent and Trademark Office.

Library of Congress Cataloging-in-Publication Data

Kaplan, Paul M., author.
  Jewish New York : a history and guide to neighborhoods, synagogues,
and eateries / by Paul M. Kaplan.
     pages cm
  Jews from Brazil arrived in New York in 1654, and a rich Jewish
history and culture continues in that city to this day. Synagogues,
eateries, museums, neighborhoods, archives, and cemeteries are
featured in this fascinating guidebook. Interviews with writers and
key figures from temples, museums, theaters, and more round out the
offerings—Provided by the publisher.
  Includes bibliographical references and index.
  ISBN 978-1-4556-1968-9 (pbk. : alk. paper) — ISBN 978-1-4556-
1969-6 (e-book) 1. Jews—New York (State)—New York—History.
2. Jews—New York (State)—New York—Guidebooks. 3. New York
(State)—New York—Guidebooks. 4. New York (State)—New York—
Ethnic relations. I. Title.
  F128.9.J5K365 2014
  917.47'10444—dc23
                            2014027488

Printed in the United States of America

Published by Pelican Publishing Company, Inc.
1000 Burmaster Street, Gretna, Louisiana 70053

To my grandparents, Sam, Gladys, Rose, and Harry, and to all immigrants who have come to America for a better life

Contents

Preface

The story of Jews in New York—it is a big subject on which surprisingly little has been written. Museums, cemeteries, archives, historic synagogues, eateries, and many places of Jewish interest are scattered throughout the city, yet few travel books have documented these neighborhood by neighborhood. Many of the stories behind these sites are largely untold.

This book seeks to change that. It highlights both the well-known and the obscure Jewish places of interest in each corner of Manhattan. It provides the background and history of each locale as well as its importance. Through these snapshots, it pieces together a little-known history of Jews in New York.

The book sheds light on facts with which many are unfamiliar. You may be surprised to learn that the first Jews came to New York from Recife, Brazil, in 1654, or that the Jewish population of New York City was very small until its exponential growth in the mid-nineteenth century, or that Harlem was a hotbed of Jewish life from the 1880s to 1920s. Perhaps you have never heard of a knish, seen a Yiddish play, or eaten an overstuffed deli sandwich. Or, alternatively, you've wanted to experience these things but haven't known where to look. Now you can discover the history, taste the food, and explore the sites that even a seasoned New Yorker may not recognize. And, of course, you'll hopefully have lots of fun along the way!

Who Should Use This Book

Whether you are a resident of New York City or the greater metro area, a tourist on vacation, or a businessperson in the city with a few extra days to spare, this book is for you—regardless of your religious or ethnic background. It is for people of all faiths and cultures, no matter your previous knowledge of Judaism or Jewish history.

Though this book focuses on the Jewish experience, its themes are largely universal. The Jewish immigration story is one strand in a fabric woven of similar experiences from people around the world. Many of the sites and museums tell stories that cultures around the world can relate to: immigration followed by social mobility, labor movement, tensions between socialist and capitalist ideologies, the need for a place of worship, and historic conservation versus gentrification.

To make the most of this book, all you need is a little interest in Jewish culture, a sense of adventure, and some imagination. Some of the buildings, such as many of the Yiddish theaters on Second Avenue, no longer exist, so you will need to imagine what it would have looked like. Some of the archival photos will help. Other sites still stand, but their function has changed, such as the former synagogues in Harlem, which are now mostly Baptist churches. As an astute observer, you can trace details that reveal a building's past. This guide will simply point out the clues.

Set forth on your journey. Walk the historic neighborhoods. Try classic dishes at the delis. Observe the beauty of the historic synagogues. Learn about the Jewish people in New York, from their auspicious arrival in 1654 to the present. This book will be your guide.

Using This Guide

The neighborhoods of Manhattan are arranged from south to north. This book will provide a bit of background and the "story behind the sites." Below are tips for you to gain the most from this book:
• Read the historical introduction! It will provide important context.
• Each neighborhood has a map for a basic visual orientation. Feel free to supplement with other maps if you need to.
• "Tips for the Visitor" feature helpful hints on planning a smooth visit to the site.
• Hours, admission prices, and subway lines change. Verify the

information on the sites' Web sites or by phone. Web addresses and phone numbers are provided.

- If hours aren't available, synagogues may be closed when you visit. You can usually gain access by attending a service or a public program.
- Kosher eateries are denoted "kosher," but check with the eatery to find out the level of Kashrut. Prices are categorized as price per entrée, excluding taxes and tip: Inexpensive, less than $10; Moderately Inexpensive, $10 to $20; Moderate, $20 to $30; Moderately Expensive, $30 to $40; Expensive, $40 or more.

Acknowledgments

I am grateful for the support of many during the completion of this project, which has been a labor of love.

Thanks to Jessica Siemens, the photographer for this book, for her effort and dedication, and to Michael Siegel, the cartographer, for making complex maps fit in this format. Thanks to Maggie Blanck for her generosity in sharing historic photos from her collection. I am appreciative of Justin Ferate for his insightful comments on the introduction. I also am grateful to Laurie Tobias Cohen for her insights and profound guidance. The Lower East Side Jewish Conservancy was very helpful in coordinating tours, providing a wealth of information, and introducing me to subject-matter experts. Other contributors include Joyce Medelsohn, Barry Feldman, and Martin Shore, who all provided invaluable content. I would like to thank Avram Gutmann of Khal Adath Jeshurun, Bonnie Dimun of the Museum at Eldridge Street, and Bryna Wasserman and Zalmen Mlotek at the National Yiddish Theatre for their content-rich interviews.

I could not have completed this book without the support of my family, friends, and colleagues. I am thankful to my parents, brother Andrew Kaplan, uncle Ted Katz, and cousins Diane and Ed Ziegman. May this book serve as an inspiration to my nephews Kyle and Julian Rozanes and their parents. I am grateful for my friend Barney Pearson and his unwavering encouragement and support. I also acknowledge the support of other friends: Jiyoung Cha, Sharon Goldman, Ron Klayman, Jacob Koskimaki, Donna Lalwani, Gregory Lucas, Sumesh Matan, Angela Pruitt, Carol Tong, and Felix Kaplan. I also wish to thank my managers, Tina Miletich, Kelly Howard, and Ben Eva, as well as my stellar colleagues on the digital team at Broadridge Financial Solutions.

I wish to thank Marian Brown Public Relations for her

outstanding efforts in publicizing the book and coordinating events as well as her colleagues Louise Crawford and Ed Velandria for social-media and Web-site consultations. I also am thankful to the staff at Gotham Writing.

I want to thank Morris Vogel, the president of the Lower East Side Tenement Museum, and New York State Assembly Speaker Sheldon Silver for providing testimonials and Deputy District Office Director Zach Brommer for his efforts.

Thank you also to the stellar team at Pelican Publishing, including the talented editor in chief Nina Kooij, promotion director Antoinette de Alteriis, and sales director Don Anderson.

Introduction

When did the Jews first arrive in New York, and where did they come from? A common misconception is that New York has always had a high percentage of Jews, mostly of Ashkenazi heritage (Central or Eastern European origin). In fact, from the early 1600s to the days of Dutch New Amsterdam in the early 1800s, Jews comprised a very small percentage of New York's population, and the earliest Jews were mostly Sephardic (of Spanish or Portuguese origin) by way of Central and South America.

The Jewish Plymouth Rock

The story begins in May 1654 in Recife, Brazil, with twenty-three "Marranos" or "secret Jews" who were fleeing from religious persecution. Most of the ancestors of the Brazilian Jews either had fled or been expelled from Spain and Portugal during the final years of the fifteenth century. Spanish law mandated that all Jews who did not convert to Roman Catholicism—some 200,000 people—were required to leave the country by July 31, 1492. When the Spanish and the Portuguese thrones joined in 1490, with the marriage of Afonso of Portugal to Isabella, the eldest daughter of Isabella I and Ferdinand II of Aragon, the Spanish Inquisition became part of Portugal's history as well.

Seeking refuge in Brazil following the Spanish Expulsion, most Jews found that their haven in Roman Catholic Brazil was tenuous. Most Jewish practices, including worship and rituals, could not be displayed openly under Portuguese rule. That all changed when the Dutch conquered northern Brazil in 1624, allowing the Marranos to finally establish the first public Jewish communities in the Americas at Bahia and Recife, yet this lifting of restrictions would be short-lived. After the Portuguese recaptured northern Brazil in 1654, they presented an ultimatum to the Jewish colonists: renounce Jewish practices and pledge allegiance to Portugal, or leave within three months.

Choosing exile over Portuguese rule, six hundred Jews of Brazil sold their belongings at substantial financial loss and sought a new refuge. The majority moved to Holland, where there was an influential colony of Portuguese Jews and where the Dutch were welcoming to the Jewish community. A smaller group sailed to the British, French, and Dutch islands in the Caribbean.

One ship, however, experienced a different fate. Headed to the Netherlands with twenty-three Jewish men, women, and children on board, the ship was captured by Spanish pirates. Then, en route to a Spanish port in the West Indies, the vessel was seized by a French privateer and towed to the French West Indies. Stranded in a strange port with almost no belongings, the refugees had no place to turn.

Their subsequent decision would mark the beginning of Jews in New York but would also burden the refugees with a tremendous debt. The French captain demanded twenty-five hundred guilders for the passage to New Amsterdam. The Brazilian Jews agreed, promising to be collectively responsible for the debt. As collateral, they agreed that all their belongings would be forfeited if the debts were not paid in full.[1] Once the "Jewish Mayflower" reached New Amsterdam, the ship's captain sold the Jews' property at a public auction. Three of the six adults were imprisoned as debtors after the sale left them still owing 495 guilders.[2]

The reaction of the Dutch colonists to the Jews' fate was mixed. Some who had bought the Jews' belongings at bargain rates returned the goods to their original owners, and some invited Jews into their own homes. While a number of Dutch colonists were hospitable to the indigent refugees, the governor of New Amsterdam, Peter Stuyvesant, was not. The governor objected to the Jews residing in his colony. Explaining that the Jewish newcomers would be a financial burden on the colony, he formally requested that the Dutch West India Company order their deportation. In his petition, Stuyvesant lamented, "It would create still great confusion if the obstinate and immovable Jews came to settle here."[3]

The Jews fired back. In January 1655, the Jews of New Amsterdam appealed to the Dutch West India Company to revoke Stuyvesant's eviction order. The Jews argued that "the more of loyal people that go to live there [New Amsterdam], the better it is in regard to the increase of trade."

The company ultimately decided in favor of the Jews. While the company acknowledged that the Jews could possibly cause difficulties, it also reminded the governor that some Jews had suffered heavy losses in Brazil out of loyalty to Holland and that other Jews in Holland were significant investors in the company. Stuyvesant was told that "these people may travel and trade to and in New Amsterdam and live and remain there, provided the poor among them shall not become a burden to the Company or to the community, but be supported by their own nation." The company later permitted Jews to trade and buy real estate in New Amsterdam. Tolerated but not entirely welcome in New Amsterdam, the Jews remained few in number. The community was prohibited from building a synagogue but allowed to create a burial ground. Sadly, this Jewish cemetery—the very first in North America—has been lost over time with no visible trace. Their second burial ground survives in part on Chatham Square.

Although permitted to stay in the colony, the immigrants endured severe limitations on their civil rights, including their right to trade, own land, and pursue various professions. The Jews pursued a second successful court action in 1655 and 1656 to lift these restrictions. The Jews, who previously had not been allowed to serve in the militia, were able to help defend New Amsterdam and were no longer required to pay onerous, discriminatory penalty taxes. Within a few years after their arrival in New Amsterdam, Jews had gained key civil rights.

By 1664, much of the Recife congregation had left Manhattan, probably because of a lack of business prospects. Most likely, they went to the Caribbean. The borrowed Torah scroll had been returned to its owners in Amsterdam in 1663. The only two Jews who remained in New Amsterdam were Asser Levy and his wife, Miriam, both Vilna-born Lithuanian Jews (Ashkenazim). The emigration of the Jewish community in New Amsterdam seemed a result of problems making a living within the economically-unstable colony. New Amsterdam was not blessed with plentiful natural resources. It lacked the cash crops of sugar or tobacco, and furs were its most profitable commodity to trade. The Caribbean promised far greater economic opportunities than did New Netherlands.[4]

Once the British took control of New Amsterdam (and renamed the town "New York"), the crown extended and expanded the rights to Jews given by the Dutch. In both the public and private spheres, Jews enjoyed additional freedoms, including the right to campaign for public office and to pray openly in a public place of worship. Historically, New York's Jews had prayed in private homes. Around 1695, but certainly by 1704, Congregation Shearith Israel was established, renting a space on Mill Street (present-day South William Street). After decades of transient spaces, in 1730 the congregation members built and consecrated New York's— and North America's—first synagogue on Mill Lane. The building of a noteworthy and public religious structure for the Jewish community was indicative of the acceptance of Jewish society by English authority.[5]

From Colonial Times to Civil War

During the period of British control, the Jewish community in New York went from winning civil rights to playing key roles in government. Some Jewish merchants collected for the British government. Others represented the colony's interests in Parliament. In 1748, Peter Kalm, a Swedish naturalist living in the colony, wrote that "Jews enjoyed all the privileges common to the other inhabitants of the town or the province."[6]

One hundred years after the first Jewish settlement, Jews numbered only about 100 out of a total population of 13,500.[7] Historic records indicate that New York's Jews had already made an impact on the city's business and civic life and established the framework of an organized community and a tradition of public service.

By the 1760s, the Jewish community in New York City had expanded nearly threefold. Still, there were fewer than three hundred Jews. The only synagogue, Shearith Israel, followed the ancient Sephardic *minhag* (ritual), despite having a majority of Ashkenazi members. On the eve of the American War for Independence, the Jewish community was split between Patriots and Loyalists to the Crown. With Jews having gained some prominence under the British colony, some worried that their status would diminish by living in an independent colony. Others believed they would obtain greater freedoms.

After the colonists won the war, new constitutions secured groups' rights. Symbolically, Gershom Mendes Seixas, the *hazzan* (cantor) and spiritual leader of Shearith Israel, was invited to participate in George Washington's first presidential inauguration. Washington presented a famous letter affirming religious freedom for Jews.

New freedoms also led to structural changes in religious organizations. In 1825, a subgroup of Shearith Israel separated and founded Congregation B'nai Jeshurun (Sons of Israel). In 1829, a group left B'nai Jeshurun to establish Congregation Ansche Chesed (People of Kindness). Another congregation spawned in 1839 after some Polish congregants formed Shaare Zedek (Gates of Righteousness). Other budding congregations at this time include Shaarei HaShamayim (Gates of Heaven) in 1839, Rodeph Sholom (Pursuers of Peace) in 1842, and Temple Emanu-El (God Is with Us) in 1845. Besides enacting organizational changes, these budding congregations faced structural accomplishments, converting existing churches to synagogues or building new synagogues. They also changed locations on numerous occasions. This proliferation of temple building was another result of increased freedoms.

New York Jewry was split in its views on slavery. Many Jews were cotton traders, and their product relied on Southern slave labor. Slavery was prohibited in New York in 1827, yet schools and theaters remained segregated. Most Jews who owned slaves freed them, but some denied their liberation until forced to do so. Some insisted that key biblical texts substantiated slavery. Others adamantly condemned it, referring to other biblical texts. Although views on slavery differed, Jewish support for the Union was overwhelmingly and consistently proactive.

Growth of the German-Jewish Population: "Rags to Riches"

Jewish immigration increased steadily in the 1820s and 1830s and reached significant numbers in the 1840s. Immigrants arrived primarily from the kingdoms of Bavaria and Posen, where Jews were subject to major restrictions and heavy taxes. Jewish immigration from Poland increased after the failed November Uprising of 1830 against the Russian Empire. Most immigrants to New York were indigent, arriving only with clothing and limited household goods. Many had their passage paid for by relatives or Jewish communities abroad. A second wave of immigration followed the 1848 revolutions in the German states and the Austrian Empire. This group of Jewish immigrants was more cultured and affluent than other groups.

By this time, New York was home to more than half of the fledgling country's Jewish population of 13,000. Jewish immigrants from various countries brought with them their cultural divisions. German Jews considered themselves superior to those from Poland, while both Germans and Poles looked down on the Galicians, Lithuanians, and Romanians, who began arriving after 1860. The established Jewish communities often feared that the new immigrants—who were generally more religiously traditional and less urban—would endanger the Jews' position in American society, which they had worked diligently to achieve. Among these various groups of immigrants, both intermarriage and burial in the same cemetery were considered unacceptable.

From the 1850s to the 1880s, many affluent German Jews left downtown and moved to what was then uptown near East 30th to East 57th streets and West 59th to West 96th streets. German Jews quickly integrated into the middle class. In the expanding post-Civil War economy, many of the peddlers, secondhand dealers, artisans, and merchants became affluent New York department-store owners, real-estate investors, bankers, industrialists, and manufacturers, including such household names as Guggenheim, Gimbel, Altman, Stern, and Bloomingdale. An example of the rags-to-riches story was that of Lazarus Straus, who arrived from Georgia deeply indebted. He was the father of the Straus brothers—Isidor,

Oscar, and Nathan—who sold the family crockery and glassware to R. H. Macy and Company. The brothers became partners in Macy's in 1888 and co-owners in 1896.

Some Jews also made fortunes from finance during this time and were philanthropic with their fortunes. Jacob Schiff, for example, a banker-turned-philanthropist, helped fund the care of thousands of needy Jewish immigrants. In 1881, when New York's major immigration depot, Castle Garden, was overwhelmed by the influx of Eastern European Jews, Ward's Island, located in the East River, became the de facto immigration depot for the Jewish refugees. To ensure adequate housing for these thousands of new immigrants, Jacob Schiff contributed $10,000 to build additional structures. The Hebrew Immigrant Aid Society (HIAS) was founded to address the pressing needs of these impoverished refugees at Ward's Island and Castle Garden.

Inspired by her rabbi, the prominent Jewish social activist Emma Lazarus came to Ward's Island to aid the Jewish refugees who were fleeing anti-Semitism and grueling poverty. It was her work with these individuals that inspired her to pen her most famous sonnet, "The New Colossus." Her words transformed the Statue of Liberty into a symbol of the immigrant: "Give me your tired, your poor,/ Your huddled masses yearning to breathe free,/ . . . Send these, the homeless, tempest-tost to me,/ I lift my lamp beside the golden door!'"

At the end of the nineteenth century, as the economy grew, wealth increased, and means of transportation expanded, some German-Jewish merchants left the crowded Lower East Side for the more serene Harlem area. The first settlement was in East Harlem, followed by a move to the more affluent section of Central Harlem around Lenox Avenue and 120th Street. There the Jews built several synagogues, the first of which was organized in 1873, Congregation Yod b'Yod (Hand-in-Hand), which survives today as Temple Israel and is located at 112 East 75th Street.

Peak of Jewish Immigration from Eastern Europe: 1880-1924

The Jewish community in New York City was predominantly

German in 1871, at which time the immigration of German Jews to the United States slowed as Jews benefitted from the newly united country of Germany and therefore the factors that fueled emigration were greatly lessened. Yet, as German Jewish immigration decreased from 1880 to 1900, Jewish immigration from Eastern Europe and Russia to New York grew exponentially. Prior to 1880, about 25,000 Eastern European Jews had reached the United States, most remaining in New York. During this time, there was an "increase of more than 23 times as many Jewish residents from Eastern Europe and Russia."[8]

These new Eastern European immigrants were generally impoverished, poorly educated, rarely fluent in English, and possessing few marketable skills for an urban environment. The majority of these new American immigrants headed to the Lower East Side of Manhattan, making the neighborhood one of the most populated on the planet at the time.

New immigrants crammed into tenements, often with five or more family members living in a small one- or two-room apartment. An observer noted that by the final years of the nineteenth century, the Lower East Side had become a "seething, human sea, fed by streams, rivulets and rills of immigration fleeing from all the Yiddish-speaking centers in Europe."

Many Jewish immigrants joined the thriving but tremendously exploitative garment industry. The clothing contractor system resulted in conditions of unimaginable squalor. "The homes of the Hebrew quarter are its workshops also," wrote Jacob Riis in his study of slum conditions. "You are made fully aware of it before you have travelled the length of a single block . . . by the whir of 1,000 sewing machines, worked at high pressure from earliest dawn till mind and muscle gives out together. It is not unusual to find a dozen persons, men, women and children, at work in a single small room." Riis was describing a typical "sweatshop."

The great influx of Jews from southern Russia in the early 1880s fueled this "sweating system." Earlier Jewish immigrants from western Poland were mostly skilled tailors, a trade that was not prestigious back home but formed a basis for relative economic well-being in America. Conversely, few of the Jews arriving from

Jewish immigrants shop for Shabbat on crowded Hester Street, one of the Lower East Side's primary areas at the time. (Courtesy Collection of Maggie Land Blanck)

Russia were skilled in the garment trades. The fundamental distinction between the Russian-Jewish immigrants of the time is that Jews from western Russia arrived in America for economic opportunities, whereas the Jews from southern Russia arrived en masse to flee from societal persecution. This exodus was, in many respects, an accidental social revolution. Men who had been affluent in Russia were reduced to penury and unskilled labor. Others, who may have been hired hands in Russia, were flourishing economically from New York's entrepreneurial jungle. These newly middle class often hired the formerly affluent. Scholars from Europe had the toughest transition because they were deemed as having no marketable skills by employers in America.[9]

Most new arrivals regarded jobs in the garment industry as a reliable income with which to save money for schooling for a profession or for the launch of their own businesses. It did not always work out that way. Some families had to take in boarders or work extremely long hours in order to save money for a child's schooling. Many immigrants could not escape the cycle of poverty, although some challenged the system to fight for a better, more equitable future.

During this period, numerous philanthropic organizations appeared. Many were started by affluent German Jews from uptown who had mixed feelings toward the new immigrants. On the one hand, German Jews were sympathetic to the desires of the new immigrants for increased economic and political freedoms. On the other hand, they were often concerned that some of the newcomers' socialist ideas and strange customs might reverse the social, economic, and cultural strides the German Jews had achieved within American society. As the famed American leader Rabbi Kaufmann Kohler wrote in 1889, "Will the Russian or Romanian Jew, now an object of pity owing to his defective education, his lack of culture, his pauperism, his utter helplessness, drag American Judaism down from the honorable position it has attained?"

Given the differences in values, a schism between "Uptown" and "Downtown" Jews emerged. While affluent Uptown Jews regarded the newly arrived Downtown Jews as "unwashed," "uneducated," and "un-American," the Downtown Jews regarded Uptown Jews as over-assimilated and in denial of their Jewish heritage. Despite these tensions, German Jews established organizations to help the newcomers. Among these agencies was the United Hebrew Charities, which provided basic help such as food, housing, aid in searching for a job, and medical assistance.

Jewish immigrants on the Lower East Side also started self-help organizations, called *Landsmannschaft* (hometown benevolent societies), and medical and burial aid societies. They also created "settlement houses," which often required that social workers live and work on-site. Examples of such societies include the Hebrew Free Loan Society, the Hebrew Orphan Asylum, the Henry Street

Settlement, Hebrew Immigrant Aid Society, and the Young Men's Hebrew Association (YMHA).

The orthodoxy of European Judaism did not always survive in the American land. Often, young people who emigrated were indifferent or even hostile to tradition. Moreover, many were drawn to the socialist values espoused by leading intellectuals such as Abraham Cahan, the co-founder and chief editor of the *Jewish Daily Forward*. The realities of an American life made it difficult to maintain an Orthodox practice. For instance, many employers insisted that employees work on Saturday. Signs read, "If you do not come to work on Saturday, do not bother coming on Monday." There emerged a social pressure from friends and family to adjust to the New World, to discard clothes, rituals, prayer shawls, and religious law. Some Jews openly defied Jewish laws by participating in previously unheard of events such as Yom Kippur balls, a lively event that severely contrasted with a holiday considered to be the most sacred and somber day in the Jewish calendar, one that demands fasting and specific prayer rituals.

Sects of religious observance became more ambiguous. Some of the previously fervently Orthodox worked on the Sabbath or attended a Yiddish theater performance on the day of rest. Conversely, some Jews who did not consider themselves Orthodox continued to keep kosher, mostly out of habit and tradition rather than from *halacha*, Jewish law.

Shuls, or synagogues, played a key role in the life of all Jews across many neighborhoods in New York. Affluent German Jews built magnificent synagogues for the budding Reform movement in Midtown, such as the Central Synagogue and Temple Emanu-El. Many aimed to rival the elaborate Christian churches through the use of stained glass windows and the incorporation of choirs and pipe organs. Some congregation members criticized these synagogues for not having enough Jewish ritual elements.

On the Lower East Side, Jews organized into *shuls* by their town of origin. Given the large number of towns, there were a great number of *shuls*. These synagogues varied greatly in size. Some organized in storefronts or in tenement flats. Others built larger structures if the congregants could afford it. Jewish religious observances typically were not lavish, so often a smaller space sufficed. Two famous

synagogues from the period, which are still operational today, are
the Bialystoker Synagogue (Congregation Bait Ha'Knesset Anshe
Bialystok) and the Eldridge Street Synagogue (Congregation Khal
Adath Jeshurun with Anshe Lubz).

Despite the struggles of immigrant Jews, many enjoyed
two forms of entertainment popular in the early twentieth
century: vaudeville and Yiddish theater. Jewish entertainers
often performed in the vaudeville style for American audiences.
Immigrant audiences loved vaudeville because it was a perfect
escape from daily struggles. Performers were on stage for seventeen
to twenty minutes with their act and included such celebrities as
Eddie Cantor and the Marx Brothers. Cultural historians observe
that vaudeville performances mimicked the rhythms of urban life.
As such, Lower East Side audiences could easily and comfortably
relate to the emotional environment of the spectacle on stage. The
comedy acts emphasized punch lines and physical comedy, and
audience members with limited English could generally follow
most of the show and be readily entertained.

Yiddish theater also provided a key entertaining and cathartic
outlet, often staging highly emotional, dramatic plays. Immigrant
audiences could relate to many of the themes. Plays consisted
of renditions of classical biblical tales, comedies about the
tribulations of immigrant life, and sentimental melodramas about
families coming to America.

Quiet Decline: 1925-1950

The 1920s saw great economic expansion across the city as a
result of heavy speculation on the stock market. These "Roaring
Twenties," however, ended with the collapse of the stock market.
By the late 1920s, Jewish immigration dramatically slowed
for several reasons. First, in the mid-1920s, the United States
Congress drastically changed immigration laws, barring most
immigrants from legally entering the United States. Second,
given the severity of the Great Depression—which hit New York
particularly hard—there were no economic incentives or factors
to attract new immigrants.

In the 1940s, the Jewish population in New York City decreased, reversing a decades-long trend. The population of the Lower East Side also dramatically fell in the 1930s. New York City's government changed the housing laws, making many of the tenements of the Lower East Side illegal.

Rather than make the costly upgrades and repairs, many landlords opted to rent out the ground level of buildings to retail stores and discontinued renting out the substandard, dilapidated floors above. The city banned pushcart peddlers, once a way of life for many immigrants. Likewise, there were fewer jobs in the Lower East Side because fewer shoppers were attracted to the area. Also the garment industry—long a mainstay of the neighborhood— had moved to Midtown West, in the area of Seventh Avenue and West Thirty-Fourth Street, near Macy's Department Store. After the prosperity and expansion of the 1920s, the harshness of the depression had a hefty negative effect on the Jewish community in New York and elsewhere. Between the two world wars, anti-Semitism increased.

At the onset of World War II, Jews in New York had heard reports by both eyewitnesses and the media of atrocities against the Jews in Europe. Some Jews in influential positions, such as Rabbi Stephen Wise, tried to convince President Roosevelt to act against the aggressors. The president's position remains highly controversial to this day. Many suggest that "he did not do all that was in his power to respond to the reports of German atrocities against the Jews of Europe. President Roosevelt had many concerns while fighting the war—among them the fear that the war would be misconstrued as a 'Jew war,' as one commentator recalled. Some blamed Jewish leaders for not applying greater political pressure."[10]

Countering the tragedies of World War II, hope within the New York Jewish community was revitalized by the convergence of religious and communal activity on the part of a third generation—primarily by Eastern European Jews. In the 1930s and 1940s, the German, Sephardic, and Russian communities in New York had begun to fuse into a native-born generation that had shared the dislocations of the depression, the sharp sting of anti-Semitism, the terrors of World War II, and the joyous pride in the rebirth of Israel. This generation is said to have reasserted Jewish identity in this country and inspired a return to the synagogue.

Religious differences, however, continued to divide the community. The differences in philosophies and rituals among sects of Orthodox, Conservative, and Reform Jews caused strife. Two political forces also divided Jews in New York as elsewhere: Zionism and communism. Each agenda raised questions about economic justice versus traditional ideas as well as obligations to Israel, a symbol around which many American Jews united.

From Decay to Renewal: 1950 to Present

In the postwar decades of the 1950s and 1960s, New York Jews generally prospered. A general increase in social status accompanied growing affluence as a result of declining anti-Semitism. With social mobility came geographic mobility, and American Jews left cities for suburbs and spread across the nation to Los Angeles and Miami. In a dramatic reversal, the Jewish population of New York began to decline. Because of the migration to the suburbs, by the 1970s, the quality of life in New York City had deteriorated substantially. With its tax base eroded, the city was in financial crisis. New York's infrastructure was crumbling. The subway system was scarred with graffiti, and many neighborhoods were perceived as dangerous. New Yorkers coped with an electrical blackout that led to significant looting and with horrors such as the Son of Sam tabloid murderer. That New York City was the setting for a number of film-noir movies in the 1970s, such as *The French Connection*, was both indicting and indicative of how much the city had deteriorated.

Many formerly Jewish neighborhoods were in steep decline during this period. Most notably, the Lower East Side saw a dramatic rise in crime as the neighborhood physically deteriorated. Many key historic structures such as synagogues, businesses, and cultural institutions were in disrepair and often vandalized. As Jewish residents departed, the neighborhood became home to a poor, predominantly Puerto Rican and Chinese community.

The City of New York, in an attempt to utilize artists to revitalize the neighborhood, sold a number of abandoned synagogues (and other structures) to such artists as Angel Orensanz, Hale Gurland, Milton Resnick, Pat Passlof, Larry Rivers (born Yitzhok Loiza Grossberg), and others. Serendipitously, many of the Lower East Side artists (including all those previously mentioned) were Jewish. New York City Mayor Edward Koch was famously quoted as saying, "The role of the artist is to make a neighborhood so desirable that the artist can no longer afford to live there." Today, the Lower East Side is home to the New Museum of Contemporary Art and numerous destination art galleries.

While the Jewish population diminished on the Lower East Side, it expanded in Brooklyn and Queens. During the 1970s and 1980s, some Soviet Jews who were allowed to immigrate to Israel actually selected other destinations, most notably the United States. While Jewish immigration from Europe declined, Jewish Soviet immigration increased significantly. Many New York Jews tried to facilitate the process for Jews leaving the Soviet Union to arrive in the US. Refugees from the Soviet Union, including Bukharians and Georgians, began immigrating in the 1980s and 1990s. Many settled in Queens and Brooklyn.

In the 1990s and 2000s, New York City transformed from urban decay to urban renaissance. Neighborhoods formerly in decline boasted new luxury apartments, stores, and services catering to the affluent. While New York had always been a tourist destination, neighborhood rejuvenation and reductions in crime have made it one of the world's leading tourist destinations, with more than 52 million visitors in 2012.

One outcome of this renaissance has been a trend toward preserving and restoring historic sites. Key Jewish buildings that were in great disrepair have been refurbished, such as the Eldridge Street Synagogue Organizations, built in the 1990s to encourage restoration and awareness of neighborhood history. Two key examples are the Lower East Side Tenement Museum and the Lower East Side Jewish Conservancy.

While restoration efforts are positive, ironically, these historic neighborhoods are threatened by gentrification itself. With land skyrocketing in value during the real-estate boom of the late 1990s and 2000s, developers have aggressively bought up property with the unfortunate result of demolishing historic structures. Poorer and middle-class residents have also been driven out as a result of sharp increases in the price of rent.

Today, the New York metropolitan area holds the largest Jewish population in the world outside of Israel. According to the United Jewish Appeal Jewish Community Study of New York, "the greater New York City metropolitan area's Jewish population is approximately 1.54 million, which increased 9 percent from 2002 to 2011. Thirty-six percent, or 561,000, of them live in Brooklyn."[11]

The Jewish community continues to play a pivotal role in New York City's government. Many of New York's recent mayors have been Jewish, including Abraham D. Beame, Edward I. Koch, and Michael R. Bloomberg. Jews are also essential providers of social services to the city. Organizations such as the United Jewish Appeal have thrived. These agencies seek to "provide access to crucial human services to all New Yorkers, whoever they are, and Jews everywhere."

It is through this community outreach that New York Jewry fulfill the demand placed on their shoulders in 1654 by the Dutch West Indies company in order to remain in what was then New Amsterdam: "These people may travel and trade to and in New Amsterdam and live and remain there, provided the poor among them shall not become a burden to the Company or to the community."

JEWISH
NEW YORK

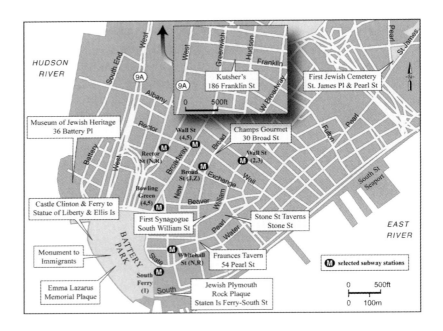

HUDSON
RIVER

Kutsher's
186 Franklin St

First Jewish Cemetery
St. James Pl & Pearl St

-N-

9A

9A

West

West

Greenwich

Hudson

Franklin

W. Broadway

South End

Albany

0   500ft

Museum of Jewish Heritage
36 Battery Pl

Rector

Wall St
(4,5)

Champs Gourmet
30 Broad St

Pearl

Fulton

Battery

West

Broadway

Rector
St (N,R)

Broad
St (J,Z)

Exchange

Wall St
(2,3)

Wall

South St
Seaport

Castle Clinton & Ferry to
Statue of Liberty & Ellis Is

Bowling
Green
(4,5)

New

Beaver

William

First Synagogue
South William St

Pearl

Water

Stone St Taverns
Stone St

EAST
RIVER

Monument to
Immigrants

BATTERY
PARK

State

Whitehall
St (N,R)

Fraunces Tavern
54 Pearl St

selected subway stations

Emma Lazarus
Memorial Plaque

South
Ferry
(1)

South

Jewish Plymouth
Rock Plaque
Staten Is Ferry-South St

0   500ft

0   100m

Pearl

St James

Lower Manhattan

Explore New York's oldest neighborhood, where the first Jewish immigrants sailed to New Amsterdam in 1654 and lived among the Dutch settlements. Now comprised of the financial district and Tribeca, experience the immigrant story from the ports of entry, Castle Garden and, later, Ellis Island. While in Battery Park, marvel at the dramatic sculpture *Monument to the Immigrants*. For a comprehensive look at Jewish history, be sure to visit the Museum of Jewish Heritage nearby. Visit America's oldest operating tavern, Fraunces Tavern, and walk by the spot that once housed the oldest Jewish congregation in the US. Stroll through the neighborhood and grab a drink at one of the refurbished historic taverns on Stone Street.

Museums

Castle Clinton Monument and Museum
Open daily 8:30 a.m. to 5:00 p.m.
Free admission
Telephone: (212) 344-7220
Web site: www.nps.gov/cacl
Subway: 1 to South Ferry/Whitehall; 4 or 5 to Bowling Green; or R or W to Whitehall Street/South Ferry

As you look at the New York harbor, think about the immigrants who came by ship into an unknown land. They were anxious and fearful, yet hopeful. The *Monument to the Immigrants* embodies their emotional state.

From 1855 to 1890, Castle Clinton would have been the port of entry for these immigrants. The Yiddish term *Kessel Garten* refers to Castle Garden. The term describes a chaotic scene of crowds of immigrants confused and unsure how to proceed. Walk around the onetime fort and observe its unique structure. Inside, look at exhibits on the building's versatile past. Look for the photos and drawings of its former uses.

Background

The worn brick, *D*-shaped structure was first built as a fort to defend the harbor before the War of 1812. Named for Dewitt

Recruiting immigrants at Castle Garden. (Courtesy Collection of Maggie Land Blanck)

Clinton, a governor of New York, this was one of five forts built to defend the harbor against Great Britain. In 1845, the military fort transitioned to a fashionable concert hall. Journals describe the interior as a "fanciful garden, tastefully ornamented with shrubs and flowers."[1] Ten years later, it was used to process immigrants. From 1855 to 1890, about 7 million immigrants passed by its walls.[2]

In 1890, the immigrant processing center moved to Ellis Island for two reasons. First, there was reported large-scale corruption at Castle Clinton. Second, the venue was not suitable for processing a high number of arrivals. At the closing of the century, as immigration rates skyrocketed, the operational efficiency of processing immigrants became a key issue.[3]

Castle Clinton changed its function yet again. The site became the New York City Aquarium until its relocation to Coney Island in 1941. Castle Clinton almost was demolished by city planners in 1946. Later, the National Park Service renovated the building to its original design. In 1975, the multipurpose historic structure reopened as Castle Clinton National Monument. Ironically, the fort once constructed to keep people out now hosts guests from around the globe.

Interesting Fact: In the mid-twentieth century, city planners often prioritized function over historical value. Many buildings were torn down—or planned to be razed—in favor of infrastructure projects. Castle Clinton was no exception. In the 1940s as part of city expansion plans, Castle Clinton was slated for destruction to make room for a second Brooklyn bridge. Fortunately, planners ultimately decided to construct a tunnel, avoiding the demolition. The connection to Brooklyn is now through Brooklyn Battery Tunnel, which runs under the building.

Fraunces Tavern
54 Pearl Street
Open every day 12 p.m.–5 p.m.
Museum Admission: $7 adults, $4 students and seniors
Telephone: (212) 968-1776
Web site: www.frauncestavern.com
Subway: 4 or 5 to Bowling Green; 1 to South Ferry; or J, M, or Z
    to Broad Street

There are not many buildings left in New York from the colonial era.
Fortunately, there is Fraunces Tavern, one of the oldest operating
taverns in the United States. Explore the museum on colonial history,
the cozy and historical tavern, and the colonial cuisine at the restaurant.

*Fraunces Tavern, on Pearl Street, one of the oldest functioning taverns
in America.* (Photograph courtesy Jessica Siemens)

A member of the wealthy De Lancey family who later owned the tavern, Oliver De Lancey, a non-Jew, married Phila Franks, a descendant of one of the original Jewish settlers in New Amsterdam. They married in secret in 1742. After six months, they announced their marriage—to their families' chagrin. In a letter, Phila's mother, Abigail, spoke of her sense of dismay and anguish. She never spoke to Phila again.

Background

The tavern began as an opulent residence in 1719 for Stephan Delancey, a businessman. In 1762, the residence became a popular tavern after Samuel Fraunces bought it. The establishment is named after Fraunces, the tavern-keeper.

The Sons of Liberty convened at Fraunces Tavern on the eve of the War for Independence. Most notably, on December 4, 1783, George Washington bid goodbye to his officers in the Long Room of the Fraunces Tavern.

Tip for the Visitor: Sip whiskey drinks at the Dingle Whiskey Bar, once cited as "the most beautiful place on earth" by the National Geographic.[4] The bar is cozy during a cold winter night with its roaring fire and location away from the crowded bar.

Museum of Jewish Heritage: A Living Memorial to the Holocaust
36 Battery Place
Museum Hours: Monday and Tuesday 10 a.m. to 5:45 p.m.,
    Wednesday 10 a.m. to 8 p.m., Thursday 10 a.m. to 5:45 p.m., Friday
    10 a.m. to 5 p.m., Sunday 10 a.m. to 5:45 p.m., closed Saturday.
Admission: $12 adults, $7 students, $10 seniors; Free
    Wednesdays 4-8 p.m.
Telephone: (646) 437-4200
Web site: www.mjhnyc.org
Subway: 4 or 5 to Bowling Green or 1 to South Ferry or Rector Street

Tucked away on the majestic Hudson River in Battery Park City, you will find the Museum of Jewish Heritage. Whereas the Jewish Museum on the Upper East Side focuses primarily on art, this museum features exhibits on Jewish history across the centuries, with an emphasis on the Holocaust. Other than exhibits, the museum is replete with symbols, including boulders in the museum's garden with saplings growing from them, representing the resilience of the Jewish community.

Opened in 1997, the museum is organized around three basic themes, each of which occupies a floor: "Jewish Life a Century Ago," which covers life in the nineteenth century until the 1930s; "The War Against the Jews," covering the Holocaust; and "Jewish Renewal," which portrays post-1945 years to the present. The museum's mission statement is to "honor those who died by celebrating their lives, cherishing the traditions they embraced, examining their achievements and faith and affirming the vibrant worldwide Jewish community that is their legacy today,"[5] and the museum accomplishes its task through the many films and exhibits. The museum provides a strong introduction to Jewish history.

Garden of Stones, a garden with eighteen boulders with saplings growing from them as a metaphor for the tenacity of life. Designed by Andy Goldsworthy. (Photograph by Melanie Einzig)

Even if you are already familiar with the subject, you will likely see and learn something new.

The building itself is symbolic, its six sides paying tribute to "the six points of the Star of David and the six million Jews who died in the Holocaust."

Abby Spilka, associate director of the museum, notes some of the unique features of the museum's setup: "The Museum's location on the waterfront of New York Harbor allows visitors to enjoy inspiring vistas of the Statue of Liberty and Ellis Island even before they encounter the Museum. We have used these icons in our *Voices of Liberty* sound installation. Visitors walk through a gallery that overlooks the harbor and listen to oral testimonies from Holocaust survivors, Soviet refuseniks, and Rwandan refugees as they talk about various themes, such as seeing the Statue of Liberty for the first time, what it was like to arrive in a new country, learn the language, or what they brought with them when they left home."

Visit some of the galleries for their spectacular views of the Hudson River. On the second floor, enter the contemplative Garden of Stones.[6] Spilka explains the deeper significance of the

Voices of Liberty, *a unique exhibit featuring oral testimonies on a variety of world events and immigration themes.* (Photograph by David Paler)

garden. "Andy Goldsworthy's *Garden of Stones* is a contemplative space dedicated to the memory of those who perished in the Holocaust and honors those who survived. For the *Garden of Stones*, Goldsworthy's only permanent installation in New York City, he worked with nature's most elemental materials—stone, trees, and soil—to create a metaphor for the tenacity and fragility of life. Eighteen boulders form a series of narrow pathways in the memorial garden's 4,150-square-foot space. A single dwarf oak sapling emerges from each boulder. As the trees mature in the coming years, each will grow to become a part of the stone, its trunk widening and fusing to the base."

Ask about the museum's original documentary films and Holocaust survivors' testimonies. Hear from many who played a role during World War II including soldiers, rescuers, and others.[7]

Tip for the Visitor: For hungry visitors, the Heritage Café is open until midafternoon most days and offers spectacular views of the Hudson River. The café serves breakfast, lunch, and snacks. The menu is somewhat limited, and the food is kosher.

Statue of Liberty
Board the ferry to Liberty Island and Ellis Island Immigration Museum in Battery Park. Follow the signs.

Open daily 9:30 a.m.–5 p.m. (last ferry departs around 2 p.m.); extended hours in summer

Free admission. Ferry to Statue of Liberty and Ellis Island: $12 adults, $10 seniors 62 and older, $5 children 4–12

Telephone: (212) 363-3200 (general info)

Web site: http://www.nps.gov/stli

Subway: 5 to Bowling Green

The Statue of Liberty is worth visiting as part of a larger excursion to the Ellis Island Immigration Museum. You have undoubtedly seen many images of the iconic New York symbol from a distance or in films, but here you have a chance to see it up close. When weary immigrants arrived at the New York harbor in the late nineteenth and early twentieth centuries, this was often their first view of the new land. No monument more vividly embodies the nation's ideals of political freedom and economic potential. Though nervous about their new, unknown surroundings, immigrants likely felt a strong sense of relief that their arduous journey across the ocean was over.

Background

Edouard René de Laboulaye, a French historian and political figure, conceived the idea for the statue. He admired American democracy and was proud of France's contribution to the formation of the budding nation. He negotiated the financing of the statue with the French government, which agreed to fund the statue if the United States provided its base. The funding for the base proved difficult. To promote contributions to the base, from 1876 to 1882 the torch-bearing arm of the statue stood in Madison Square Garden. Tourists were interested in viewing the unique structure but not necessarily contributing. Then, the renowned publisher Joseph Pulitzer trumpeted the cause in his newspaper, the *New York World*; funds flowed in. In 1883, as part of the fundraising effort, New York poet Emma Lazarus, a Sephardic Jew, agreed to compose a poem related to the statue. She was intimately involved with efforts to assist Russian pogrom victims, which influenced the tone of her poem.[8] At the base of the statue is a plaque bearing her sonnet "The New Colossus," of which the most widely known lines are "Give me your tired, your poor,/ your huddled masses yearning to breathe free."

The statue was displayed to the public on October 28, 1886. It was fabricated from 100 tons of copper and more than 125 tons of steel. It took ten years to complete the pedestal upon which the statue stands.[9]

Ellis Island

Hours: The first boats of the day leave the mainland (Battery Park, New York/Liberty State Park, New Jersey) at 9:30 a.m. Last entry into the security tent is 3:15 p.m. Longer hours during the summer. Final ferries of the day leave Ellis Island at 5:15 p.m.

Museum Entrance Fees: None, but ferry prices are $13.00 for

adults over 13, $10.00 for seniors 62 and over, and $5.00 children 4–12

Ferry tickets can be obtained *only* from the Statue Cruises ferry company, in one of three ways:

1. Call 1-877-LADY-TIX (1-877-523-9849)
2. Online at: www.statuecruises.com
3. Same day at the ferry ticket box office in Castle Clinton in Battery Park, New York City, or at Liberty State Park in New Jersey

Web site: www.ellisisland.org/genealogy/ellis_island.asp

Immigration has always been a vital thread in the history and development of the United States. Few places embody that better than Ellis Island.

Ellis Island replaced Castle Clinton as the primary venue for processing immigrants arriving in New York harbor in 1892, though the present building opened around 1900. Ellis Island has a mythic status in stories of American immigration and is the subject of many books and films. For many immigrants, it meant a new opportunity in a nation full of hope. But it was also a frightening place for many. No immigrant was guaranteed admission into the United States, even after making the often-grueling, costly journey across the ocean. Upon arriving at Ellis Island, immigrants were "processed"—they were examined for contagious diseases, financial status, and likelihood of surviving in the new country. Many did not speak English, so exchanges were often difficult.

Eastern European Jews faced a special problem, since they could not eat non-kosher food. The Hebrew Immigrant Aid Society (HIAS) aided arrivals with mediators and interpreters. In certain cases, they helped the newly arrived find employment and shelter.

Ellis Island served as the immigrant processing station until 1954. Its function significantly changed after 1924, when the National Origins Act placed tough restrictions on immigration. According to the Ellis Island Web site, "The venue took on the additional role of a detention and deportation processing center.

During World War II, it was used to intern those suspected of espionage or sabotage."[10] When immigration laws relaxed in the mid-1960s, the processing of immigrants fundamentally changed. Thus, newer waves of immigrants, including Latin American, African, and Asian immigrants, usually have few ties to Ellis Island.[11]

The museum was closed for many months following the October 2012 damage from Hurricane Sandy, but it is once again open to the public.

Tip for the Visitor: The same ferry leaving Battery Park goes to the Statue of Liberty then arrives at Ellis Island, so you can visit both sites in one trip. The Statue of Liberty and Ellis Island Tours are very popular, and there may be long lines or large crowds during your visit. To make your trip more enjoyable:
• Get an early start! The first boats leave at 9:30 a.m.
• Book your tickets online beforehand to avoid long lines.
• Be prepared for security checks.

There are four excellent, self-guided exhibits showcasing the social and cultural roles of Ellis Island in the lives of immigrants:[12]
1. Journeys: The Peopling of America, 1550–1890, which profiles the immigrant experience before Ellis Island opened in 1890 and explores immigration issues then and now
2. The American Flag of Faces, which shows visitors' photos collected in a flag image
3. The American Immigrant Wall of Honor, which lists the names of immigrants on a wall
4. The American Family Immigration History Center, which provides research of your family history if they came through Ellis Island

Immigrants walking through inspection stations at Ellis Island. (Courtesy Collection of Maggie Land Blanck)

Tip for the Visitor: To find the best research about your ancestor's arrival through Ellis Island, do your homework before you visit. Try to find out key information such as full name, approximate age at arrival, and whether he or she traveled with others.[13]

Places of Interest

Emma Lazarus Memorial Plaque
Battery Park
Subway: 4 or 5 to Bowling Green; or 1 to South Ferry

The plaque is dedicated to Emma Lazarus (1849-87), a descendant of the first Sephardic Jews who arrived in New Amsterdam in September 1654. Donated by the Federation of Jewish Women's Organizations, the plaque features Lazarus's historic 1883 sonnet "The New Colossus," which is inscribed at the Statue of Liberty.

The text is poignant and evokes the feeling of hope and yearning of immigrants.

Jewish Plymouth Rock Plaque
State Street, opposite the Staten Island Ferry Terminal
Subway: 1 to South Ferry

Amidst today's hustle and bustle of commuters going back and forth to Staten Island is the area where the first Jewish settlers arrived. To commemorate their arrival, a plaque near the front of the ferry station reads, "Erected by the State of New York to honor the memory of the twenty-three men, women and children who landed in September 1654 and founded the first Jewish community in North America."

About ten feet away is a sculpture of a map from colonial New Amsterdam. Take a look at the layout so you can see how houses and buildings were positioned. Notated is "Slick Street" or "Mud Street," which was a part of one of the earliest Jewish communities.

Monument to the Immigrants
Next door to Castle Clinton
Subway: 4 or 5 to Bowling Green; or 1 to South Ferry

Immigrants arriving to the new land were frightened and confused, yet optimistic—they were entering the "Golden Land." Their trip on the ships was arduous and often painfully long. The *Monument to the Immigrants* captures this mixture of emotions.

The monument honors the brave men and women who sought a better future. Some of the figures in the foreground are wearing *yarmulkes* (pronounced "YAH-muh-kuh), or head coverings. The figures in the sculpture express a range of emotions. Some show happiness and relief, while others show trepidation. The monument was sculpted by Luis Sanguino, cast in 1973, and dedicated in 1983. The inscription reads, "Dedicated to the people of all nations who entered America through Castle Garden, in memory of Samuel Rudin, 1896-1975, whose parents arrived in America in 1883."

The monument captures the emotionally exhausted immigrants as they passed through Castle Garden and entered a new land. Sculpted by Luis Sanguino, it was cast in 1973 and dedicated in 1983. (Photograph by Jessica Siemens)

Emigrants about to board a ship in hopes of new opportunity. (Courtesy Collection of Maggie Land Blanck)

First Jewish Settlement on Mill Lane
Between Stone and South William Street
Subway: 2, 3, 4, or 5 to Wall Street

Visit the location of the first Jewish settlement. One of the shortest streets in New York City, Mill Lane is little known even to the savviest New Yorkers. It was first laid out in 1657 and was known as Ellet's Alley until 1664.

Background

The first Jewish immigrants from Recife, Brazil, were not permitted to build a synagogue. Their stay in New Amsterdam was precarious, as the governor of the colony, Peter Stuyvesant, protested their arrival by petitioning the Dutch West Indian Company to evict the Jews. Once the British defeated the Dutch a decade later, policies on practicing religion became more liberal. Tracing the first synagogue's location is tricky because much of the practice was underground. Historical records indicate that services were hosted in private houses in the 1690s. The informal congregation became formalized around 1706 as Shearith Israel. About two decades later, in 1730, the congregation built a synagogue at this location.[14]

City records indicate that around this time there were about thirty Jewish families in New York City. According to the American Jewish Historical Society, "the synagogue was expanded and rededicated in 1818." Mordecai Manuel Noah, a playwright, proclaimed, "Until the Jews can recover their ancient rights and dominions, and take their rank among the governments of the earth, this is their chosen country; here they can rest with the persecuted from every clime, protected from tyranny and oppression, and participating of equal rights and immunities."[15]

Eventually, the expanding congregation moved north to a new building on Crosby Street, where they worshipped from 1834 to 1860. Visitors of today's Shearith Israel building can view historic artifacts from the original synagogue.

Interesting Fact: The street is named after the seventeenth-century mill industry in New Amsterdam.

Oldest Jewish Cemetery
St. James Place near Chatham Square
The cemetery is usually closed but you can view it from outside the gate.
Subway: J, Z, 4, 5, or 6 to City Hall, then walk east along Park Row to St. James Place

Cemeteries are hard to find in Manhattan. Nevertheless, the tombstones remaining there offer a glimpse into the past. Shearith Israel (also called the Spanish and Portuguese Synagogue), the first congregation in New York, consecrated this cemetery in 1683. In the area of today's Chinatown, it is the oldest cemetery in the United States with a Jewish population. Though the cemetery opens to the public only once per year, peer through the gates at St. James Place and imagine some of the early congregants of Shearith Israel.

First cemetery of the Spanish and Portuguese Synagogue, or Shearith Israel, from 1656 to 1833. (Photograph by Jessica Siemens)

Background

Records show that the first Jewish cemetery in the US was constructed around 1656 in New Amsterdam,, "where authorities granted Congregation Shearith Israel a little hook of land situated outside of this city for a burial place. Its exact location is now unknown. The congregation's second cemetery, which is today known as the first cemetery because it is the oldest surviving one, was purchased in 1683."[16]

The Foundation for the Advancement of Sephardic Studies and Culture provides the history of the cemeteries:[17]

"1st Known Cemetery: 55 St. James Place, opposite Chatham Square, in use 1682–1828
2nd Known Cemetery: 76 W. 11th, between 6th and 7th Avenue, in use 1805–1829
3rd Known Cemetery: 21st Street between 6th and 7th Avenues, in use 1829–1851"

Visitors can see all three cemeteries from outside the gates.

Buried in this cemetery, Walter Jonas Judah is a tragic yet heroic figure.[18] Judah was the first native-born Jew to attend medical school, which he began at seventeen years old. During September 1798, historic records indicate "an average of 38 New Yorkers per day expired from yellow fever."[19] As a result, well-off New Yorkers fled the city. But Walter Jonas Judah had other goals—he wanted to stay and help the sick. He was said to pay out of his own pocket for medications for those who could not afford them. Ultimately, he perished alongside his patients. The young man who strove to combat deadly viruses himself succumbed to the yellow fever outbreak at the young age of twenty.

Part of the inscription on his tombstone reads, "In memory of Walter J. Judah, student of physic who, worn down by his exertions to alleviate the sufferings of his fellow citizens in that dreadful contagion that visited the City of New York in 1798, fell a victim to the cause of humanity on the 5th of Tishri 5559 [September 15, 1798]."[20]

Historic Synagogues

Site of North America's First Synagogue, Shearith Israel
South William Street; no landmark exists, but currently there is
   a Lincoln Square Parking Garage
Subway: 2 or 3 to Wall Street; or J or Z to Broad Street

Though there is no physical structure to see here, you can witness the location where the first Jewish community in New York worshipped on South William Street (originally called Mill Street) in a rented house until the first synagogue was erected in 1730.

Civic Center Synagogue ("Floating Synagogue")
49 White Street
Web site: www.synagoguefor thearts.org
Subway: 1 to Franklin Street

You probably have never seen a synagogue like this one. Because of the structure's architecture (it looks like a wave), the structure "floats" next to the street. Located in Tribeca, the Civic Center Synagogue, designed in 1967, is nestled between two former sweatshop loft buildings. Its design is intended to remind the viewer of a spread-open Torah scroll. Unlike most modern synagogues, there are no interior windows, only skylights. The building remains one of the unique architectural wonders of New York City's modern synagogues.

If possible, enter the synagogue to see the unique interior.

Background

Constructed for an Orthodox congregation in 1967, the Civic Center Synagogue historically catered to workers in the textile industry as a weekday synagogue since its inception in 1938. In 1957 the synagogue stood at 80 Duane Street downtown for convenience.[21] In the mid-sixties, the congregation was displaced and erected a new synagogue during the architectural experimentation of the 1960s.

Conservation literature notes the symbolism of the unique structure: "The bowing façade imitates the shape of the burning bush flame, while the windowless sanctuary is lit from a skylight high above the bimah." These elements create the building's enigmatic quality.

Eateries

Champs Gourmet Deli
71 Broadway and 30 Broad Street
Price: Inexpensive
Telephone: (212) 363-2100
Web site: www.champsdelinyc.com
Subway: 2, 3, 4, or 5 to Wall Street

This very informal eatery offers standard deli fare. Try the grilled roast beef, fresh mozzarella on toasted garlic bread, and pea soup.

David's Kosher
40 Exchange Place
Kosher
Price: Inexpensive
Telephone: (212) 248-9008
Subway: 2 or 3 to Wall Street

This relaxed kosher restaurant offers sushi, including special rolls such as a sweet potato tempura roll, as well as deli sandwiches such as the breaded chicken cutlet sandwich. Try the knishes and the blueback salmon platter.

Fraunces Tavern Restaurant
54 Pearl Street
Price: Moderate
Telephone: (212) 968-1776
Web site: www.fraoncestavern.com
Subway: 4 or 5 to Bowling Green; 1 to South Ferry; or J, M, or Z to Broad Street

The main reason to dine at Fraunces Tavern is the richness of its history. The tavern-like feel is cozy and harkens back to another era. The fare, which is hearty and not finicky, puts a contemporary spin on classic Irish and American dishes. Try the colonial-style shepherd's pie or whiskey-cured salmon on toasted scout bread with horseradish cream.

Next to the restaurant is a historic bar and a lounge with a fireplace, a nice place to enjoy a drink.

Kutsher's
186 Franklin Street
Price: Moderately Expensive
Telephone: (212) 431-0606
Web site: www.kutsherstribeca.com
Subway: 1 to Franklin Street

Kutsher's strives to recall the "Catskills cuisine" inspired by Kutsher's Country Club, founded in 1907. The menu, created by

Mark Spangenthal, takes a "playful approach to the canon of Jewish cooking, from small bites to more substantial offerings."[22] Sample traditional Eastern European Jewish dishes with a modern twist such as Mrs. K's Matzo Ball Soup, the pastrami-smoked salmon, or the wild halibut gefilte fish. The menu also offers "the works," including choices of Kutsher's pastrami, smoked veal tongue, duck pastrami, and other options. "Noshes for the Table" include crispy potato latkes, chopped duck, and chicken liver.

Background

The story of the restaurant mirrors the journey of many immigrants, from humble beginnings to established places in society. The Kutshers were tailors, a common profession in their Lower East Side neighborhood. They bought farmland in Monticello, where they hosted summer visitors. During the busy days of the 1920s, small bungalows and hotels sprung up in the Catskills. In subsequent decades, the small lodging facility became a notable Catskills destination resort. In the 1950s, the family expanded the facilities, and it became frequented by celebrities such as Billy Crystal, Joan Rivers, and Rodney Dangerfield. Musical talent such as Duke Ellington performed there as well.

In more recent decades, vacationing in the Catskills has declined. But for many, fond memories remain. The current generation of the Kutsher family, along with business partners, is trying to revive these remembrances through this restaurant. Kutsher's recently announced plans to relocate. A new location is still being sought.

Lenny's Café
108 John Street
Price: Inexpensive
Telephone: (212) 385-2828
Web site: www.lennysnyc.com/
Subway: 2 or 3 to Fulton Street or Wall Street

This is an informal, self-service deli. It is perfect for a quick lunch to go on an action-packed day of sightseeing. Many rave about the chicken sandwiches and freshly breaded chicken cutlets.

Pita Express
15 Ann Street
Kosher
Price: Moderately Inexpensive
Telephone: (212) 571-2999
Web site: www.pitaexpressnewyork.com
Subway: 2, 3, 4, or 5 to Fulton Street

Pita Express is an informal Middle Eastern/Israeli kosher eatery with
table service. Try the chicken soup, avocado and eggplant hummus,
or a "spicy hot-dog shawarma." The atmosphere is relaxed.

Stone Street Taverns and Restaurants
52 Stone Street
Telephone: (212) 785-5658
Web site: www.stonestreettavernnyc.com
Subway: 2 or 3 to Wall Street; or J or Z to Broad Street

*Stone Street Tavern and other eateries along the historic Stone Street, a
stone's throw from the location of America's first synagogue, Shearith Israel.*
(Photograph by Jessica Siemens)

On this historic, tucked-away street, you will think you have left Manhattan as you gaze at the cobblestone streets and northern-European architecture.

There are several taverns and restaurants from which to choose on Stone Street. While none serve Jewish cuisine, they offer the chance to experience an atmosphere similar to what early Jewish settlers would have known. In the warmer months, the restaurants have extensive outdoor seating.

Try the Stone Street Tavern for a drink, pub food, and quaint, exposed-brick, candlelit interior.

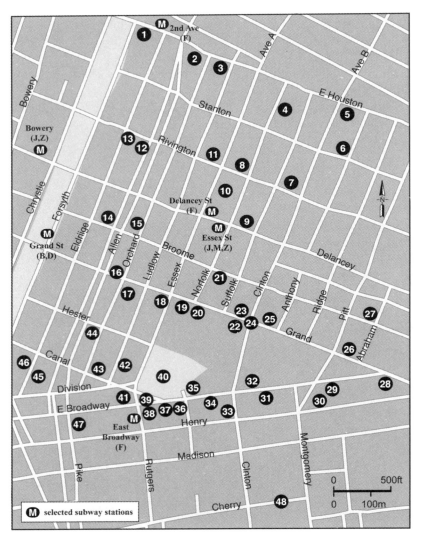

See legend on page 58

Lower East Side

Explore one of the country's most vibrant and colorful neighborhoods: a place that has shaped America. Once the most densely populated neighborhood in the world, the Lower East Side has been home to immigrants from around the globe. Visit the illuminating and newly restored Eldridge Street Synagogue, and spend an afternoon at one of the nation's best history museums, the Tenement Museum, where immigrant stories come alive. And be sure to try a knish from Yonah Shimmel, a pastrami sandwich from Katz's, and the famed lox from Russ and Daughters. Amidst this trendy modern neighborhood, you will find echoes of history on every street.

Museums

Museum at Eldridge Street
Located in the Eldridge Street Synagogue at 12 Eldridge Street
    (between Canal and Division)
Open Sunday-Thursday 10 a.m.–5 p.m., Friday 10 a.m.–3 p.m.
Admission: $10 for tour or self-guided tour; free on Mondays
Telephone: (212) 219-0888
Web site: www.eldridgestreet.org
Subway: F train to East Broadway; or B or D to Grand Street; or
    6, N, Q, R, J, or Z to Canal Street

Eldridge Street Synagogue is one of the most beautiful synagogues in New York City. Its survival of the tumultuous changes in the neighborhood over the last century is a testament to the efforts of urban and cultural preservationists. In today's vibrant Chinese neighborhood, standing next to a popular Buddhist Temple and

Legend to Page 56 Map

Museums
45 Museum at Eldridge Street
15 Tenement Museum

Places of Interest
4   Angel Orensanz Foundation
48 Early Home of Irving Berlin
34 Educational Alliance
10 Essex Street Market
25 Site of First Convention of
   Workmen's Circle
38 Former Garden Cafeteria
26 Harry De Jur Playhouse
33 Founding Site of Hebrew Free
   Loan Society
30 Henry Street Settlement
46 Home of Eddie Cantor
43 Jarmulowsky's Bank Building
37 Jewish Daily Forward Building
32 Jewish Mural
42 Former Kletzker Brotherly Aid
   Association
17 LES Business Improvement
   District Visitor Center
24 LES Jewish Conservancy
   Visitor Center
41 Former Loew's Canal Street
   Theater
28 Mikvah
39 Nathan Straus Square
36 Newspaper Row
12 Former Public Bath
40 Seward Park

35 Seward Park Branch, New
   York Public Library
9   Site of Ratner's
16 Former Site of Ridley's
   Department Store
8   Former Schapiro's Koshery Wine
29 Shteeble Row
7   Streit's Matzo Factory
31 United Jewish Council
13 University Settlement House

Historic Synagogues
27 Bialystoker Synagogue
23 Site of Congregation Emanu-El
21 Beth Hamedrash Hagadol
5   Congregation Chasam Sopher
14 Congregation Kehila Kedosha
   Janina
44 Former First Roumanian-
   American Synagogue
47 Former Pike Street Shul
6   Stanton Street Shul

Eateries
20 Doughnut Plant
11 Economy Candy
3   Katz's Deli
19 Kossar's Bialys
22 Noah's Ark Original Deli
18 Pickle Guys
2   Russ and Daughters
1   Yonah Shimmel Knish Bakery

Eldridge Street Synagogue. Photograph by Kate Milford. (Courtesy Museum at Eldridge Street)

bubble tea outlet, it harkens back to the days when the neighborhood—one of the most densely packed in the world—was the center of Jewish life. Cross the street to see a wider view of its magnificence. Its round arches, rose window, and decorative motifs strike every pedestrian walking by. The architecture conveys the interior's sense of tranquility amidst the hustle and bustle of the busy city.

The establishment has two parts, run separately: the synagogue and the Museum at Eldridge Street.

Eldridge Street Synagogue

A common practice in the late nineteenth century was for newly emerging congregations to purchase churches up for sale, particularly Methodist congregations heading for uptown. Smaller congregations often acquired one-room storerooms. However, the congregation at Eldridge Street Synagogue built the structure itself. It is consequently called "the first immigrant-built synagogue in the United States," erected in 1887.

In the 1850s, a small congregation of Russian and Polish immigrants gathered in makeshift spaces in various locales on the Lower East Side to form the congregation that would build Eldridge Street Synagogue. Its founding members include Isaac Gellis, of hot dog fame, and Sender Jamulowsky, of Jamulowsky's Bank.

When the building was completed, observers admired the magnificent architecture. This distinctive place of worship was significantly different from the majority of synagogues on the Lower East Side. Its architecture was more grandiose, its demeanor more sedate. It offered a respite from the crowded streets and dilapidated tenements. For some, it represented the opportunity to have a peaceful life.

The prominence of its staff matched its opulent exterior. The celebrated Pinchas Minkowsky was brought from Odessa, Russia, to serve at the High Holidays. The preeminent cantor commanded the immense sum of $15,000 per year, an unheard-of amount at the time.

The synagogue also functioned as a melting pot for people from different economic segments of society. Peddlers, sweatshop workers, established merchants, entertainers, and key religious figures worshiped side by side. Besides worshiping, some congregants used the community to help find jobs and housing. Also, while many synagogues at the time had congregations from a particular town, Eldridge Street Synagogue's congregation drew from the entire home region of the Eastern European immigrants.

The history of the synagogue's congregation largely parallels that of the neighborhood—a story of thriving participation during the immigration boom in the early decades of the 1900s, followed by a dramatic drop in participation, to its rediscovery and renewal in the closing decades of the century. At the turn of the twentieth century, over one thousand worshipers came to services, but by the 1940s much of the Jewish population had moved away, and services were moved to the basement. By the 1950s, more members left the area, and immigration quotas restricted new immigrants into the country. As the sanctuary began to show serious wear and tear, including leaks, the congregants closed it off. Left without funds to adequately keep up the sanctuary, congregants worshiped downstairs in the smaller house of study (Beth Midrash). From 1955 to 1980, the main sanctuary was not used.

Then the crumbling sanctuary was reinvigorated, thanks to the efforts of a professor at New York University. In 1971, while conducting a survey of Jewish landmarks in the Lower East Side, Gerard Wolfe had been intrigued by this structure. He contacted the caretaker and gained entrance into the synagogue, only to find a rickety staircase, fallen debris, and crumbling walls. He recalls that moment: "My first thought was that I had somehow entered 'The Twilight Zone' and had been transported in time." Professor Wolfe initiated the landmark designation process and formed the Friends of Eldridge Street Synagogue, a group that fundraised to refurbish the basics of the decrepit synagogue. He organized the Synagogue Rescue Project, whose mission was to save the historic synagogue.

In the mid-1980s, a new group, the Eldridge Street Project, facilitated by Roberta Brandes Gratz and William Josephson, began the daunting task of restoration. Returning the synagogue to its original glory was painstaking and aimed for authenticity rather than a sanitized version of the past. This approach led to the retention of indentations in the pine floorboards from decades of worshipers *davening* (praying in a traditional rocking motion).

The restoration took twenty years and cost about $20 million. Bonnie Dimun, executive director of the Museum at Eldridge Street, notes, "What is so remarkable about the restoration is its authenticity. It looks like it did in 1887. Developers carefully consulted the documentation of what the original building looked like to ensure its authenticity. For example, when you walk in the sanctuary, you can feel the footprints of the early users of the synagogue. The floors are original. The chandeliers are original."

The only contemporary component is the stained-glass window

above the ark, made by artist Kiki Smith and architect Deborah Gans. In the 1940s, the original window was badly compromised, and glass blocks were put in as placeholders. There was a financial decision to make: pay off the mortgage or put in a new glass window. They chose the former. But in 2010 a new window was installed. The documentation did not include the specifications of the original window, so restorers had a decision: match the new window to the front one or create something to represent the future? They chose the latter. The synagogue that journalist Bill Moyers once called a "landmark of the spirit of an ancient people on a new exodus, and the spirit of a new nation committed to the old idea of liberty" was returned to its glory.

During the twenty-year restoration period, there were continuous worship and events. Today, services are open to any members of the public who would like to pray in an Orthodox service.

Museum at Eldridge Street

After the Lower East Side's Jewish population declined in the mid-twentieth century, membership at the synagogue declined markedly as well. During the reconstruction of the Eldridge Street Synagogue, the Museum at Eldridge Street was founded to tell the remarkable story of this historic structure.

Programs are aimed at the general public and tell the synagogue's history as well as the larger immigration history. Executive Director Bonnie Dimun notes, "This is the story of all new immigrant groups who come to a new land and try to retain some cultural elements."

Tours tell the story of the synagogue, including its beginnings and recent renovations. The tours explain the difference between beautifying the synagogue and preserving it. They lead groups to the main sanctuary and explain its symbolism. Even if you are not familiar with Jewish rituals and practices, you will not be confused on this tour. It defines terms. Other highlights of the tour include viewing pictures before the renovation and touring the women's balcony.

For a tour focused on the architecture or on Jewish ritual, consult the Web site or inquire at the ticket desk. Occasionally there are tours with those focuses. Also inquire about walking tours of the neighborhood. For children, ask about the monthly "Preservation Detectives Family Tour," which teaches kids about restoration, stained glass, and finding objects of significance.

Tip for the Visitor: If you are visiting the Lower East Side in June, find out when the annual Egg Rolls and Egg Creams festival is and join one of the city's most innovative block parties, a side-by-side showcasing of local Jewish and Chinese communities. Enjoy the juxtaposition of traditions: Chinese opera, cuisine, mahjong, acrobatics, and calligraphy along with Challah baking, klezmer music, Yiddish language lessons and songs, and synagogue tours.

Lower East Side Tenement Museum
108 Orchard Street
Open daily 10 a.m.–6 p.m.
Admission: $25 for adults per tour; discounts for members
Telephone: (212) 982-8420
Web site: www.tenement.org
Subway: J or Z train to Bowery Street; walk three blocks east on Delancey Street to Orchard

Whereas most historic homes tend to concentrate on wealthy individuals, the Lower East Side Tenement Museum honors those most often forgotten by history: the everyday people. It tells their stories. The museum allows you to trace former tenants' footsteps as you visit their restored homes. You will see objects that were part of their daily lives and listen to recordings of former residents and their descendants.

It is a must-see for any social-history enthusiast. The museum offers several distinct tours showing the lives of families who resided at nearby 97 Orchard Street from 1860 to 1930. Each of the following tours runs several times per day.

"Hard Times" focuses on a German Jewish family in the late nineteenth century whose patriarch went missing during the Panic of 1873. The tour raises interesting questions about social mobility and inheritance rights. It also features an Italian Catholic family who survived the Great Depression. In a poignant tape recording, one former resident recounts her memories of the tenement.

"Sweatshop Workers" portrays a Jewish family's garment workshop and home in the late twentieth century, when the Lower East Side was the most densely populated place in the world. The tour raises questions about balancing work, family, and religion during an explosive time. The tour explores the tough choices religious families had to make, such as keeping their jobs by working on Saturdays or preserving the Sabbath, a day of rest according to traditional Jewish law.

"Irish Outsiders" depicts the Irish Catholic Moore family in the 1850s, who lament the death of a child. The tour raises key questions about public health during that period. Irish music and culture of the newly arrived immigrants is also shared. The tour also features the Russian Jewish Katz family, who lived in an improved dwelling in the 1930s.

"Meet Victoria Confino" is a historical reenactment whereby you "meet" and interact with a Greek Sephardic resident of the tenement from the early twentieth century, Victoria Confino. This tour is particularly recommended for school-age children, though adults will also find it instructive.

"Exploring 97 Orchard Street" is a unique behind-the-scenes look at curation and historical interpretation. Offered only on Thursdays, it describes historical developments in the building, including its changes due to housing legislation passed at the turn of the twentieth century.

"Shop Life" is a new tour exploring merchants at or near 97 Orchard Street. The tour explains the changes in commerce, from the German saloon of the 1870s patronized by the largely German immigrant population, to kosher butchers, to the clothing discounters on Orchard Street from the 1970s and 1980s.

If you want to discuss what you view, try the "Tour & Discussion," where you can not only attend the tours but also reflect on what you have seen with other visitors. These usually run once per day.

Walking Tours

Besides the tours of the restored tenements, the museum offers three walking tours.[1]

"Outside the Home" is a walking tour of what the Lower East Side was like from about 1880 to 1935, covering some of the sites mentioned in this chapter. What makes the tour special is that you will see the sites from the perspective of the immigrants of the period. One hour and thirty minutes, for ages eight and up.

"Then and Now" continues where "Outside the Home" leaves off, covering roughly 1935 to the present in the Lower East Side neighborhood. You will learn about the neighborhood's decline in population after the change in tenement laws, the increase in its Puerto Rican population, its dramatic decay in the 1970s and 1980s, and its subsequent boom in the late 1990s and 2000s. You will learn about the pros and cons of gentrification and witness the dynamic combination of the old and the new. Two hours, for ages eight and up.

"Food Tour" is usually offered only on Fridays and Saturdays. Explore the multiethnic cuisines of this historic neighborhood. You will sample knishes, German soft pretzels, Chinese dumplings, and Dominican fried plantains. This tour is a window into different cultures through their food. Jewish food and culture are discussed. Two hours, for ages eight and up.

The Unique Story of the Museum's Beginning: The museum had an unlikely beginning. Ruth Abram, a historian and social activist, wanted to showcase the story of the people who had lived in the tenements but found that most museums focused on the history and politics of the city or region and ignored the everyday lives of residents. Seeking to correct that, she searched for a suitable tenement in New York to convert to a museum.

The search was proving fruitless until one day Abram and her cofounder Anita Jacobson came upon the tenement at 97 Orchard Street. Initially, the pair considered using the space as a storefront starting point for neighborhood tours, but while she was looking for the bathroom, Jacobson discovered clues of the past. The toilets were from the late nineteenth century, and the wooden banister was obviously aged. Jacobson recounts the moment: "It was as though people had just picked up and left. It was a little time capsule. . . . I called Ruth and said, 'We have got to have this building.' It was perfect."[2] She had found the ideal place for the museum.

The tenements had been virtually untouched for about fifty years. This was a double-edged sword. On the one hand, they were a goldmine for historical archives. On the other hand, they were in shambles and needed significant renovations to convert them into a historic museum suitable for visitors. Researchers combed through dwellings to compile historic anecdotes about the tenants.

The museum opened in 1992, with the first restored apartment being the 1878 home of the German Jewish Gumpertz family. The museum has since restored several others.

Places of Interest

Take the time to stroll the neighborhood as you search for these places of interest. Note the clues to the past found in the architecture, which reveal the economic choices landlords made during the days of the tenement building. Barry Feldman, historian and New York tour guide, explains, "Cornices were mass-produced and became cheap to buy. So landlords would purchase them to increase the curbside appeal of the apartment. It adds character to the apartment building. It also served a practical purpose to divert rain water away from the building. Along with the cornice, terra cotta and molds were also used to create faces, floral arrangements, and other designs to create the appearance of something elite. By the 1880s and 1890s, this became common on the Lower East Side." He notes that landlords pursued this course so that prospective tenants, seeing an attractive building, would pay higher rents. The insides of the buildings, however, were often dingy and uninviting.

Amalgamated Dwellings
504–520 Grand Street (near Williamsburg Bridge)

The Amalgamated Dwellings were about bringing light—literally— to a jam-packed neighborhood plagued by unhygienic and substandard conditions. In the most densely crowded neighborhood in the world, the Amalgamated Clothing Workers Union of America built cooperative apartments to bring much-needed improvement to housing standards. Amalgamated Dwellings offered apartments with what would have been seen as luxuries at the time: new appliances, private bathrooms, and abundant light and air. The municipal projects of the 1920s in Hamburg and Vienna inspired the Hungarian architect of the Amalgamated Dwellings. Transitioning industrial spaces into residential ones, the co-ops were constructed in 1930-31 on the site of the demolished R. Hoe Printing Company, a manufacturer of printing presses.

Ironically, the site of the progressive housing movement was on the very spot that, thirty years earlier in 1902, was the scene of a tense confrontation among Jewish mourners at a funeral, non-Jewish factory workers, and the police. The exact cause of the conflict is unknown. In a nutshell, about 25,000 mourners walked in a funeral procession for their revered rabbi. When they passed the Hoe factory, workers allegedly began to taunt them and throw objects from upper-story windows. Enraged, some mourners charged the building. Many were injured and subsequently arrested. Those involved with this racial altercation could never have known that on this exact site, some thirty years later, harmony would come from this new kind of economic experiment in housing.

Bialystoker Home for the Aged
228 East Broadway
Subway: F train to East Broadway

Looking at the front of this former nursing home, you will notice something unique. Unlike any other site in the neighborhood, this one features art deco lettering. Surrounding the entranceway are the symbols for the twelve ancient tribes of Israel.

Immigrants from Bialystok, Poland, opened Bialystoker in 1931, during the Great Depression. The home served the elderly until 2011. Citing financial difficulties, it ceased operations.

The building's subsequent fate was strongly contested between two parties. The owners wanted to sell the building. Historic preservationists vigorously lobbied for landmark status to protect its unique art deco exterior. The debate played out in front of community boards, elected officials, and landmark commissions. On May 21, 2013, the NYC Landmarks Preservation Commission formally declared the building a landmark.

The building that once symbolized the Bialystok immigrants

and their concern and care for their elderly became a symbol for historical conservation in an ever-changing and newly gentrified neighborhood.

Reputed Home of Eddie Cantor
19 Eldridge Street (between Canal and Division)
Subway: F train to East Broadway; or B or D train to Grand Street; or 6, N, Q, R, J, or Z to Canal Street

Across the street from the magnificent Eldridge Street Synagogue lived a young Eddie Cantor. The exact address is unknown, but this is the approximate location of the home of the famous actor born Izzy Iskowitz, the son of Russian immigrants. Cantor's was a rags-to-riches story. He was a charismatic, entertaining kid who performed in front of crowds in the neighborhood. At age thirteen, he debuted in *Little Lord Fauntleroy* at the Educational Alliance (see below). Cantor successfully transitioned from neighborhood star to Hollywood star, and by the early 1930s he was one of Hollywood's highest-paid actors.[3]

Cantor came to prominence in an era when many entertainers rose from poverty on the streets of the Lower East Side to fame in vaudeville, films, or the theater. Performers such as George Burns and Sophie Tucker enjoyed similar success. Eddie Cantor died in 1964 at the age of seventy-two.

Educational Alliance
197 East Broadway
Telephone: (212) 780-2300
Web site: www.edalliance.org
Subway: F train to East Broadway (between Clinton and Suffolk)

The Educational Alliance served as a meeting point between assimilated, affluent uptown German Jews and more ethnic, poorer, recent Jewish immigrants. The uptown German Jews sought to establish programs to help immigrants integrate into American life. Their motives were probably twofold. Certainly they felt a sense of compassion and, in some cases, religious obligation, but they were also motivated by a fear that the huge influx of their fellow Jews with strange, Old World customs would jeopardize their own newly found societal positions.

Accordingly, in 1889, German Jewish philanthropists, including banker Jacob Schiff and Macy's cofounder Isidor Straus, established one of the earliest settlement houses. A November 1891 *New York Times* article announced the opening of the new building.[4]

Known as the Downtown Hebrew Institute, the organization combined the services of three groups: the Hebrew Free School Association, the Aguilar Free Library Society, and the Young Men's Hebrew Association. In 1893, it was reorganized as the Educational Alliance, offering basic classes and programs on becoming a "good American," which were held throughout the day and into the evening. A library was also provided that was the forerunner of the Seward Park Branch of the New York Public Library.

The alliance offered other creative outlets to relieve the pressures of cramped tenement life. Classes in art, music, literature, philosophy, and theater were presented. Icons such as Mark Twain and Sholem Aleichem read from their works. Eddie Cantor first performed here. Radio and TV pioneer David Sarnoff learned to speak English in these classes. In 1895, the alliance established one of the first community-based art schools in the nation. The school offered instruction to children and immigrant workers in painting, etching, and drawing. Mark Rothko, one of the greatest painters of the twentieth century, was affiliated with the school.

As a response to the changing population of the Lower East Side in the 1940s, the organization introduced new social-service programs. Several of them sought to ameliorate teenage delinquency.

Today, the alliance also offers youth development programs in sports, music, and education. Recently, contestants from NBC's hit show *The Voice* judged talent-show participants. Other programs are aimed at senior citizens.

Essex Street Market
Essex Street between Rivington and Delancey
Open Monday-Saturday 8 a.m.–7 p.m., Sunday 10 a.m.–6 p.m.
Admission: Free
Web site: www.essexstreetmarket.com
Subway: J, M, or Z train to Essex; or F or V to Delancey

A staple of the Lower East Side's culinary scene, the Essex Street Market traces its roots to the 1920s. During that era, streets were filled with peddlers with pushcarts who sold everything from used clothing to furniture or housewares to eggs, chickens, or vegetables. These open-air markets that operated from early in the morning until late at night reminded the immigrants of their homelands. The chaotic scene is often portrayed in art and literature set in this densely packed neighborhood during this time. Pushcarts were an equal-opportunity employer in their day; immigrants with little money and little English could start one. By 1900, there were more than 25,000 pushcarts in the area.[5]

In the 1930s, Mayor Fiorello LaGuardia wanted to remove the peddlers. Store owners backed this effort, lobbying for the elimination of pushcarts in order to remove competition and reduce street congestion. Ironically, the removal of pushcarts hurt stores' business, as shoppers missed the experience of outdoor markets and perceived store prices to be higher. Some shoppers no longer frequented the area. Peddlers were forced to bring their business inside into the newly built Essex Street Market. Unfortunately, many could not afford the weekly fees and had to shutter their businesses.

Essex Street Market has changed along with the neighborhood. In the 1930s and '40s, the primary customers were Italians and Jews. In the 1950s, as many Puerto Ricans moved into the neighborhood, the market added stores selling Latino-style foods and goods. During the neighborhood's steep downturn in the late 1960s and '70s, the market declined, and its management was privatized in 1992 in an attempt to revive business. The effort was not successful, and control was transferred to the city.[6]

More recently, as the neighborhood has been revived and then gentrified, the market has flourished anew. Today, it houses more than twenty-five vendors, ranging from old-timers to newcomers, selling cheese, produce, and seafood. It embodies the old and the new of the Lower East Side, offering inexpensive groceries for residents and gourmet food for the seasoned cook or tourist. Check the market's Web site for special events such as cooking demonstrations or wine tastings.

Near the entrance, look for the pictures on the wall of the early days of the market.

Former Garden Cafeteria (Now Wing Shoon Restaurant)
165 East Broadway
Subway: F train to East Broadway

Today, it looks like one of many Chinese restaurants in the neighborhood. But this spot has historical significance. It was home to the Garden Cafeteria, the legendary neighborhood institution where political activists and observers exuberantly debated the issues of the day. It was, of course, before the Internet. Patrons in cafés actually had conversations with each other instead of interacting through electronics.

The who's who of Jewish thinkers gathered at the Garden Cafeteria, a kosher dairy from 1941 to 1983. From dawn until late in the evening, the 240-seat dining room was crowded with intellectuals, socialists, poets, journalists, and other neighborhood residents, usually seated at communal tables. The Garden Cafeteria was significant because prominent Yiddish journalists would argue with each other there. Isaac Bashevis Singer's short story "The Cabalist of East Broadway" captures the essence of this unique literary café. It was also a key place for older people to congregate.

Emma Jacobs, on the Web site "Places that Matter," a joint project of City Lore and the Municipal Arts Society, quotes accounts of the famed neighborhood eatery: "Customers came in and took a ticket as they entered from the man who sat on a high stool by the revolving door. The man behind the counter punched the ticket with the price of each dish the patron ordered so that the customers, who often lingered for hours, could pay for everything they had ordered at once when they finally departed."[7]

A former waiter recalled with a tone of annoyance, "They'd have a cup of coffee and they'd sit and they'd sit and they'd talk. Around about eleven o'clock the lunch hour would start to start and they'd come in. And you needed the table and they wouldn't get up. So I would go around with a wet rag and wipe the tables down so it was wet so they couldn't lean down on anything, and literally push them out, because the lunch was so fabulous here we needed a table. And then as soon as the lunch was over, they were back. The cafeteria was filled from early morning until past midnight."

Stories abound about the occupational diversity of the customers, who included local businessmen, Yiddish theater actors, writers, union activists, and older patrons. But the Garden Cafeteria closed in May 1983. Since then, it has been the Wing Shoon restaurant, serving Cantonese-style food. The name translates to "everything comes easy and fluidly," which the management says refers to the process of immigrating to America.

Although the site's ownership has changed, the symbolism of immigrants thriving in the new land remains.

Harry De Jur Playhouse of Henry Street Settlement (Originally Grand Street Playhouse)
Also referred to as Abrons Arts Center
466 Grand Street (corner of Pitt Street)
Telephone: (212) 598-0400
Web site: www.abronsartcenter.org
Subway: F train to East Broadway

Across the street from the Henry Street Settlement (see below), you will notice a theater that presents experimental dance, drama, and music. If possible, catch a performance at this historic playhouse.

The theater's history follows the pattern of wealthy uptown German Jews helping to bring culture to the impoverished immigrants. Philanthropist sisters Alice and Irene Lewishohn, who came to Henry Street as volunteers in 1911, bought a piece of land at the corner of Grand and Pitt streets. They founded the Neighborhood Playhouse in 1915, which emphasized the unconventional and abstract theater for which the playhouse eventually became known. It produced plays that showcased the cultural vibrancy of its neighborhood. One of the early "little theaters," it presented new works by classic playwrights such as George Bernard Shaw, James Joyce, and Eugene O'Neill. Later, it was renamed for benefactor Harry De Jur.

Today, the playhouse, which is part of Abrons Arts Center, serves as the dramatic and visual arts wing of Henry Street Settlement. Recent performers include Philip Glass, Lou Reed, and John Zorn.

Founding Site of the Hebrew Free Loan Society
203 Henry Street (demolished)
Subway: F train to East Broadway

The Hebrew Free Loan Society of New York, which once occupied this site, embodied the communal spirit of helping immigrants or those in need of capital for individual or business needs.

The tenement that stood at this site was converted into a synagogue in 1892 by Polish Jews. Later, it merged with a congregation from Vilna, Lithuania. During the synagogue's first year, Yiddish-speaking immigrants organized the Hebrew Free Loan Society of New York at this site.

Their aim was to assist the needy with small, interest-free loans. The founders were carrying out a *mitzvah* (good deed) and *gemilut chasadim* (bestowing acts of loving kindness). The mission embodies the philosophy expressed in the Middles Ages by Moses Maimonides of Spain: "A loan is better than charity, for it enables one to help oneself." Interest-free loans are considered a high act of goodness because they often promote opportunity and potential over handout and dependence. The project started with $95 and was supported by capital funds from Jacob Schiff, Adolph Lewisohn, and other Jewish philanthropists. In 1975, the synagogue was destroyed by arson and replaced by a six-story apartment house.

The Free Loan Society continues today at 675 Third Avenue, providing interest-free loans totaling almost $200 million to about 860,000 borrowers for education, housing, adoptions, and job retraining.[8] The focus is on ultra-Orthodox and Russian Jews, half of whom are estimated to live in poverty. The society notes that the payback period ranges from twenty months to ten years and that the default rate is less than 1 percent.

Henry Street Settlement
263–265 Henry Street
Web site: www.henrystreet.org
Subway: F train to East Broadway

Henry Street Settlement is one of the most important sites for public health. To this day, it has influenced the nursing profession. Learn the story behind this remarkable institution and, if possible, schedule a tour. If you have the time, you may even be able to participate in a community-service project with them.

Background

The buildings of the Henry Street Settlement date back to the agricultural days of the eighteenth century on the Lower East Side, when modern-day blocks were plots of farmland. The three red-brick row houses stand on what was the Henry Rutgers farm. Number 265 is closest to its initial form: built as a two-story structure, it retains its original windowsills and hand railing.

Its story begins with a courageous and determined middle-class German Jewish nurse, Lillian Wald (1867–1940), who demonstrated the extent to which one person can effect great change. While not a household name, she may be one of the most influential characters from this era.

Born into a middle-class, professional family, Lillian Wald studied at the New York Hospital School of Nursing. Then a single event changed her life. A young girl approached her one day and asked her to accompany her to a tenement to visit someone who was ill. Wald followed the girl to a squalid two-room tenement that housed more than ten people, including a family and boarders. There she decided that her life's work would be helping the poor. She moved to a red-brick row house at 265 Henry Street and cofounded the Nurse's Settlement, which became the Visiting Nurse Service and the now-famous Henry Street Settlement, often providing medical care free of charge.

Lillian Wald is often viewed as a heroine of her day, someone who wanted to ease the pain of the struggling immigrants. She frequently explained her motivation by asking a simple question: "Have you ever seen a hungry child cry?"[9]

It was a common practice for outside nurses to teach hygiene to the immigrant population. So what made Lillian Wald different from the others? The answer is that Wald took it a step further by encouraging volunteers to live in the places they served. She moved into the neighborhood (hence the word "settlement") and offered healthcare on a sliding scale. In addition to teaching hygiene, she organized educational, cultural, and recreational activities for the community. Through her work with the local population, she became a nationally recognized advocate for improved working conditions and better houses and schools. She was a champion for civil rights many decades before that movement blossomed.

Wald's devotion paid off. The Henry Street Settlement, with the help of backers such as Jacob Schiff, grew significantly. Its Web site notes that it "had seven buildings on Henry Street and two satellite centers, with 3,000 members in its classes and clubs and 92 nurses making a staggering 200,000 visits per year."

The Henry Street Settlement thrives today, carrying on Wald's legacy. As the immigrant population has largely shifted from Jews, Italians, and Irish to Chinese and Latinos, the settlement has offered community benefits ranging from transitional housing for the homeless to programs for youth. Support services include a mental-health clinic, arts center, senior center, two workforce development centers, and housing. In the decades since Wald's death, the organization has pioneered the model of combining social services with shelter for homeless families. This model offers a more holistic approach to social services.

> Tip for the Visitor: If you are traveling in a group, consider a tour offered on the second Tuesday of every month from 10:30 to 11:30 a.m. Tours are free, but advance registration is required. To register, call (212) 766-9200. Also inquire about any short-term or long-term volunteer opportunities if you are interested.

Site of Early Home of Irving Berlin
330 Cherry Street (between Clinton and Montgomery) (demolished)
Subway: F train to East Broadway

Born in Russia as Israel Isidore Beilin, the famed songwriter Irving Berlin (called "Izzy" in his childhood) emigrated with his family to the U.S. when he was about five. He lived in a modest dwelling at this site with his parents and five siblings. His father worked as a kosher poultry inspector and part-time house painter, and his mother was a midwife. Young Izzy dropped out of school at fourteen and left home.

Destitute, he began a tenuous musical career singing pop songs on street corners and in saloons. Later, calling himself "Irving Berlin," the budding songwriter worked in the historic Tin Pan Alley and then went on to the glamor of Broadway and Hollywood. His most popular songs are a far cry from his Jewish immigrant past and embody the values and dreams of his newfound country. They include such legendary songs as "White Christmas" and "God Bless America," which debuted in 1938 and was popularized on the *The Kate Smith Show* in 1960. Berlin strove to compose songs that were simple. He had said that his aim was to "reach the heart of the average American," whom he referred to as the real soul of the country.[10]

Jarmulowsky's Bank Building
54–58 Canal Street (at Orchard Street)
Subway: F train to East Broadway

This noted twelve-story bank, built in the Beaux Arts style, tells a cautionary tale of financial ruin and its devastating effects on an immigrant community. It signifies the rags-to-riches story of a successful entrepreneur followed by the riches-to-rags saga of his irresponsible descendants. It also shows the consequences of having virtually no protection for bank depositors in the days prior to the Great Depression.

The building is named after an immigrant financier, Sender Jarmulowsky. He started out in business by speculating in ticket selling—taking advantage of different ship-ticket prices in varying markets, a form of arbitrage in his day. Jarmulowsky would purchase high-volume, highly discounted steerage tickets during low season and then sell them on the open market on credit for a large profit.

In 1873, Jarmulowsky immigrated to New York and opened a business selling tickets to immigrants looking to procure tickets for their relatives in Europe. The lucrative and cash-rich business soon became a bank.

That same year, he established his private bank targeted

at immigrants. The building housing it was erected in 1912. According to legend, Jarmulowsky wanted the building to be the tallest in the neighborhood. The legend goes that he was trying to outdo the nearby Jewish Daily Forward Building (see below), because of that publication's opposing socialist bent.

The bank was a one-stop shop for immigrants who wanted to conduct business in Yiddish. Many were reluctant to hand over their savings, which they had toiled for, without knowing whether their deposits would be safe—concerns that would later prove valid. Immigrants began to trust the bank and its founder, and it became a household name.

Sender Jarmulowsky passed away not long after the completion of the bank building. His heirs acquired the bank, and this marked the beginning of the downfall of the prominent bank. Jarmulowsky's sons ran the business into the ground. Rumors of insolvency spread. Panicked, depositors withdrew their money, leaving the bank undercapitalized. In 1914, at the start of World War I, many of the firm's depositors made emergency withdrawals to assist their relatives in the Old World. Thousands protested in front of the bank. According to the *New York Times*, "Five hundred people stormed the house where son Meyer Jarmulowsky lived, forcing him to escape across tenement rooftops. Jarmulowsky's sons were indicted for banking fraud."[11] The bank shut its doors. Because this was before the days of deposit insurance (FDIC), the closure left the depositors with no money. The state of New York seized and auctioned off the bank's assets in May 1917.

In 2009, the Landmarks Preservation Commission granted it landmark status. Currently used partially for commercial activities, the largely vacant building is slated to be converted into a luxury hotel.

Jewish Daily Forward Building
173–175 East Broadway
Subway: F train to East Broadway

Stand across the street and observe the remarkable detail in this historic building that once housed the most influential Yiddish newspaper in the country. Thanks to the building's landmark status, its details still exist in the present condo complex and recall its past.

The structure is topped with a clock with Yiddish letters spelling out *Vorwartz* ("Forward"). Four busts of socialist heroes—Karl Marx, Friedrich Engels, Karl Liebknecht, and Ferdinand Lassalle—confront anyone who enters the building. It is ironic that a statue of Marx greets residents daily at what is now one of the priciest condo buildings in New York.

The Forward Building was more than the headquarters of an influential Yiddish newspaper. In many ways, it was a visible symbol of advocacy and opportunity for immigrants. It was also the center of intellectual debate and community. Various Jewish social and benevolent societies, including the Workmen's Circle, used the meeting rooms and offices. The Folksbiene (The People's Stage), a Yiddish-language troupe, utilized space in the building for more than two decades.

Located on what was known as "Yiddish Newspaper Row," the Yiddish-language newspaper *Jewish Daily Forward* had its offices in this handsome building. Other newspapers nearby included

Forward Building, once part of "Yiddish Newspaper Row" and former home of the famed socialist newspaper Jewish Daily Forward. (Photograph courtesy Jessica Siemens)

Yiddisher Tageblatt (*Yiddish Daily Paper*), *Wahrheit* (*Truth*), *Der Tag* (*The Day*), *Morgen Zhurnal* (*Morning Journal*), and humorous weekly *Der Groisser Kundess* (*The Big Stick*). But the progressive, socialist-oriented *Jewish Daily Forward* was the best known. First published in 1897, it was largely under the direction of the famous Abraham Cahnan.

The *Forward* was more than a newspaper. It was a "how-to guide" for struggling immigrants. It included articles that were in many ways forerunners of advice columns. More than a neutral reporting publication, the *Forward* advocated for its readers. It told them that they should expect more, such as more livable housing and more humane working conditions. The paper encouraged immigrants to take advantage of the night classes and cultural centers in their neighborhood. It also provided hope and entertainment.

The *Forward* encouraged a two-way relationship with its readers. It invited them to write in about topics that were troubling them, and then editors would provide timely responses. The concept was incorporated into "*Bintel Brief,*" or "Bundle of Letters," a column that answered readers' questions. Editors acted as social workers of sorts, addressing topics that ranged from religion to government to education to women looking for husbands who had abandoned the family, a common problem during this time. Other topics were less serious, such as a reader who asked whether he should be concerned about marrying a woman who had dimples in her cheeks.

As the decades wore on, the newspaper's subscribers dwindled due to fewer Yiddish speakers, more assimilation, and fewer Jewish immigrants. Also, in the 1970s, the once-thriving intellectual neighborhood rapidly deteriorated. In response, the *Forward* moved to Midtown in 1974. In 1990, an English edition was added, followed by a Russian one. The paper still operates today, but it contains more mainstream Jewish news and features and no longer reflects the socialist bent of its storied past.

The iconic building itself has gone through many changes since the *Forward*'s departure in 1974. Many of these changes seemingly contradict its Jewish and socialist past. First, the Chinese Alliance Church acquired the historic structure for $99,000. The exterior would be left largely untouched other than the addition on the western wall of large Chinese characters that translate to *Jesus leads the way.*

In the early 1980s, the building changed hands again, sold to Chinese businessperson Mui Hin Lau for around \$316,000.[12] It was sold again about two decades later, and the interior was renovated into ultra-luxury condos. To some, there is an irony in the later history of the building—what once housed socialist thought and journalism became a residential complex affordable only to a privileged few. But its past is not soon forgotten. Each day as residents enter the condo, they are greeted by the haunting figures of four socialist heroes.

Newspaper Row

Newspaper Row was home to about five major newspapers. The most famous was the socialist *Jewish Daily Forward.* The *Day* was a modern paper that reported the news. It was apolitical and secular. *Morning Journal* usually portrayed the religious aspect of immigrant life. *America's Voice* was a communist paper. It was very supportive of the Soviet Union. *Vor Height* was like the *Day.* It was secular and more cultural in nature.

> Interesting Fact: The *Day* hired Sholem Aleichem and paid him an enormous sum. He was a very popular writer because of how he depicted shtetl life in Europe. Known for writing the Tevye series, as well as other important short stories full of other characters, he was paid \$100 per week. Subscriptions rose dramatically. But after four months, the subscriptions leveled off. So he was laid off and went to work at the *Vor Height* for a considerably lower compensation.[20]

Former Kletzker Brotherly Aid Association—A Landsmannschaft
5 Ludlow Street

Across the street from the former Canal Street Theater is the former Kletzker Brotherly Aid Association, a three-story building constructed in 1892 by a group of Jews from the city of Kletzk. The organization served as a *Landsmannschaft*, an association of people who provided funds and social support to new immigrants from their hometown. Members received assistance with finances, employment, housing, medical care, and Jewish life events such as burials. Other "brotherly societies" aided small businesses or congregations.

Barry Feldman, historian and New York City tour guide, explains the background of the *Landsmannschaft*. "There were groups of people from the same city in Eastern Europe. Naturally, these people were looking to find similar food and customs as what they had back home. So the purpose of the *Landsmannschaft* was for a group to provide services to new immigrants from that group."

Typically, the *Landsmannschaft* would have an office, sometimes with a synagogue attached. Members paid dues and in exchange received key benefits such as finding relatives, networking, employment leads, and dispute resolutions with management. Unlike other social services, this was connected to the immigrant's particular dialect and hometown.

This *L*-shaped structure today serves as a Chinese funeral home.

Former Loew's Canal Street Theater
31 Canal Street (at East Broadway)
Subway: F train to East Broadway

Nestled behind a shuttered electronics shop on Canal Street is a former three-story, 2,270-seat movie theater built in the Spanish baroque style.[13] Terra-cotta ornamentation decorates the front of the building. This late 1920s movie house offered immigrants much-needed respite from their arduous tenement life. Eddie Cantor, who grew up blocks away, premiered his film *Forty Little Mothers* here in 1940. The theater became a venue for indie films, closed in the late 1970s, then housed an electronics store. Now the store has closed and the un-landmarked building's future is unknown.

A *New York Post* article noted that an Asian-American nonprofit group, Committee to Revitalize and Enrich the Arts and Tomorrow's Economy (CREATE), hopes the building will become

The former Loew's Canal Street Theater, once popular with movie-going immigrants on the Lower East Side, is currently vacant, but there are long-term plans to renovate it as a cultural center. (Photograph by Jessica Siemens)

the "Lincoln Center of Chinatown," converting the sleeping giant of a performance space into a new cultural center. The building's owners are supportive of the plan. CREATE president Amy Chin commented on the future of the former movie house. "We have a vision of this as a town square, with a store, a visitors' bureau, theaters, a café and rehearsal spaces."[14]

Interesting Fact: Chin and her nonprofit group knew of the theater but could not find its entrance. "We knew there was a theater there somewhere, but we had no idea of how to get in," she said. The mystery was solved when a longtime resident pointed them to the entrance at 31 Canal Street. Once inside, Chin said she was stunned to see so much of the 1926 theater's ornate terra-cotta design still intact. "The theater is in surprisingly good shape," remarked Guido Hartray, an architect with the firm Rogers Marvel.[15]

Lower East Side Jewish Conservancy Visitor Center
400 Grand Street
Telephone: (212) 374-4100
Web site: www.nycjewishtours.org
Subway: J, M, or Z train to Essex Street

The Conservancy is probably best known for its tours throughout New York City that focus on Jewish culture and history. You can join a public tour or arrange one on your own with up to ten people for about $150 total. Tours are led by Conservancy-trained guides, most of whom are professional educators. Some are third-generation Lower East Side residents and also state-licensed guides. What makes these tours unique is their depth and the fact that they often bring visitors inside key sites. Check the Conservancy's Web site for tour information and the most up-to-date pricing. Also inquire about any programming such as readings, exhibits, or lectures.

Background

The Conservancy was started by the United Jewish Council in 1998 in response to damage to the nearby Congregation Beth Hamedrash Hagadol after a window blew in. The rabbi reached out to the Council for funds to restore the synagogue. The Council realized that this was the tip of the iceberg, for many synagogues in the area needed repair.

The idea behind the Conservancy was to have an organization that would aggregate funds to preserve historic synagogues. Funds were raised on behalf of the sacred sites, as well as for the Stanton Street Shul; Kehila Kedosha Janina, the *shtiebel* or house of prayer on East Broadway; and Community Synagogue on East Sixth Street.[16]

Tours emerged as a byproduct of this relationship with the synagogues. They began as "insider's tours," as participants were granted rare views of the historic synagogues' interiors.

Laurie Tobias Cohen, executive director of the Lower East Side Jewish Conservancy, notes that the Conservancy strives to show the interiors of places that are off the beaten path. In many cases, a local expert, such as a synagogue leader or a university student, leads the tour. Tours span the neighborhoods of Manhattan, with new ones launched in Washington Heights, the Upper East Side, and the Upper West Side. In Brooklyn, they cover Greenpoint and Williamsburg.

Besides programs aimed at adults, the Conservancy offers an innovative educational curriculum for kindergarten through twelfth-grade students. Their signature program, the "Life of an Immigrant Child," seeks to provide a bridge between the stories of immigrants more than a century ago and the lives of current students, many of whom are also immigrants—or children of immigrants—themselves. To date, the program has served 2,000 children from the metro area. Fourth graders, for example, tour the Bialystoker Synagogue, view historic East Broadway, look at photos, purchase pickles, and more.

Mikvah of the Lower East Side
311–313 East Broadway (corner of East Broadway and Grand Street)
Telephone: (212) 475-8514
Subway: F train to East Broadway

Built as a community center, this striking Beaux Arts building is the last remaining *mikvah* or ritual bathhouse on the Lower East Side, having served the Jewish community since the 1940s.

The building has taken on different functions since its 1904 opening but has always served the general purpose of improving immigrants' social and religious lives. Constructed by the Young Men's Benevolent Association at a cost of $35,000, the five-story building contained a library, gym, club rooms, a bowling alley in the basement, and an assembly hall.

In 1919, a time when many buildings were converting to settlements, this building was acquired by Arnold Toynbee House, a settlement aimed at providing opportunities to poor immigrants. "It formed a kindergarten, provided showers, founded a summer camp, and organized a cooperative milk station. In 1924, it changed its name to Grand Street Settlement."[17]

During World War II, the building's function changed from social and educational to ritual. It became a *mikvah*, a purification bathhouse required by Orthodox Jews. Its documents describe the changes: "Installed on the first floor were 4 pure-water pools, each holding 700 gallons of rainwater collected on the roof of the building then drained through a special filter system and led through earthen pipes to the individual pools. Eight bathtubs and 4 showers were also provided."[18]

In 1996, the building was renovated under strict rabbinic supervision. Today, it is used by men in the morning and women in the evening. Although many *mikvah'ot* once speckled the Lower East Side, this is now the only one.

Mural
232 East Broadway, on the east side of the Bialystoker Home for
    the Aged
Subway: F train to East Broadway

Walking down East Broadway, you will notice a colorful and image-rich albeit decaying mural. Created by teenagers from Young Israel Synagogue in 1972, the striking mural depicts many chapters of Jewish life. See how many you can decipher.

The mural's themes are summarized by the umbrella phrase:

Mural created by teenagers from Young Israel Synagogue in 1972 with the inscription: Our Strength is Our Heritage. Our Heritage is Our Life. The painting depicts the rise of the labor movement, the Holocaust, the founding of Israel, and the plight of Soviet Jewry. (Photograph by Jessica Siemens)

Our Strength is Our Heritage. Our Heritage is Our Life. On the left, newly arriving immigrants are entering the "Golden Land" of America. Below them is the masthead of the *Forward*, showing the prevalence of Yiddish. A worker toils away in a garment factory while unions such as the International Ladies Garment Workers demand improved labor conditions. The anguish of the Holocaust is pictured at the top center. The figures behind bars symbolize the suffering of Soviet Jewry, a key issue when the mural was created. The massacre at the 1972 Munich Olympics is also depicted. Switching from cultural and political messages, the mural includes religious themes, with Shabbat candles and a prayer shawl.[19]

The mural was completed by a dozen sixteen- to nineteen-year-olds under the direction of local artist Susan Green. The entire project took about nine months.

Nathan Straus Square
Intersection of East Broadway, Essex, Canal, and Rutgers
Subway: F train to East Broadway

Inspector tests milk supply at grocery on the east side of New York. (Courtesy Collection of Maggie Land Blanck)

Walking past the small space at the intersection of East Broadway, Essex, Canal, and Rutgers streets, you may not realize that this square was the scene of several historic events. This wedge-shaped island was formerly referred to as "Rutgers Square," a nod to Henry Rutgers, a patriot and landowner whose farm covered much of this area. In the late 1800s, Rutgers Square became a focal point for social movements within the immigrant community. It was the scene of lively debate, impassioned speakers, protests about capitalism, and union rallies.

In 1931, the space was renamed "Straus Square" in honor of German-Jewish philanthropist Nathan Straus, one of the sons of the family that owned Macy's and the Abraham & Straus department store in Brooklyn. Straus was active in causes to alleviate poverty. His greatest legacy was establishing a safe milk supply through pasteurization, dramatically cutting down on infant mortality. According to the Lower East Side Jewish Conservancy executive director Laurie Tobias Cohen, he not only provided the solution but set up milk wagons so that mothers could purchase clean and wholesome milk for their children.

Former Public Bath
133 Allen Street
Subway: F or M train to Second Avenue; or B or D to Grand Street

Most nineteenth-century Lower East Side tenements had either no or limited bathing facilities, causing hygiene problems that led to higher mortality rates. Social reformers rallied for public baths, not only to ameliorate the physical condition of the impoverished dwellers but also improve their moral character. Indeed, cleanliness was viewed as leading to inner strength and therefore better citizenship among the new immigrants.

The problem was acute. An 1896 survey showed that there was one bathtub in the Lower East Side for every seventy-nine families.[21]

Before public baths, there were publicly financed outdoor floating baths. These were wooden structures that enclosed pools of river water. But pollution was a problem, which led to the establishment of an indoor public bath system. The New York

Association for Improving the Condition of the Poor (AICP) was instrumental in promoting private bath sites.

In 1901, the first municipal bathhouse was created, the Rivington Street Bath, at this location. It was renamed the "Dr. Simon Baruch Public Bath" in 1917, after a Jewish immigrant from Prussia (near modern-day Poland) who strongly advocated for public baths. In the 1940s, the building was converted into a recreation center, and it was closed in the mid-1980s.[22]

In 1992, the bathhouse was sold at city auction to a Chinese congregation with roots in Fujian province in China. The interior has been refurbished into a sanctuary. Because the building is not landmarked, it may be demolished or significantly altered.

Site of Ratner's
138 Delancey Street

Patrons recall this restaurant's excellent, quintessential Jewish food—and impertinent wait staff. They recount memories of the "hot gefilte fish, pierogies, vegetarian chopped liver, poached salmon in aspic, kasha varnishkas, and onion rolls."[23] Ratner's was more than a restaurant. It was a destination. Meyer Lansky and Bugsy Siegel often dined at the Delancey location. Entertainers who frequented the restaurant included Walter Matthau and Groucho Marx.

The famed Jewish kosher dairy restaurant closed in 2004 after eighty-six years at this location. It was founded in the early twentieth century, as Jewish immigration into New York was skyrocketing. Jacob Harmatz and his brother-in-law Alex Ratner, for whom the restaurant is named, initially opened its doors on nearby Pitt Street. After thirteen years, the restaurant moved to its Delancey Street location, where it remained until its closing. A second Ratner's opened on Second Avenue but has also closed.

Today, the space is a Sleepy's Mattress store. Sadly, there are no pictures or remnants of its storied past. Yet its memory lives on in television. Harking back to its 1960s days, Ratner's was a setting on the "Christmas Waltz" episode of the critically acclaimed TV series *Mad Men*. The episode was originally broadcast on AMC on May 20, 2012, and is available on iTunes and Hulu Plus.

Site of E. Ridley's & Son Department Store
319–21 Grand Street (near Orchard Street)

Amidst the crowded streets, the dark tenements, and the sea of peddlers stood the elegant Ridley's Department Store. Edward Ridley opened a small dry-goods shop at this location. In 1874, he replaced it with an impressive multistory building designed in a French style with a corner clock tower. After expanding further in the 1880s, it became one of the largest retail establishments in the nation. An 1886 article in the *Brooklyn Magazine* celebrated it as "one of the most stupendous and enduring edifices in the known world." The target market seemed to be bargain-hunting customers. Ridley's ads in the *New York Daily-Tribune* dubbed it the "Grand Street Cheap Store."

A *Tribune* article in 1876 delineated a variety of merchandise, such as "spring rockers, oilcloth, waffle irons, bronzes, and clothing; if you were moved by the constant singing of the loveliest canaries on the second floor, one could be yours for $2.50."[24] Store selections ranged from household articles to women's and children's clothing. Innovative for its time, the store published a fashion magazine and operated a mail-order catalog, which served as the e-commerce channel of its day.

In *Gateway to the Promised Land*, Mario Maffi recounts the store's importance in immigrant life. Even then, fashion made a statement. Immigrants looking to increase their status and call attention to their Americanization would often purchase more expensive accessories, such as hats, to signal their improved standing. Maffi calls such purchases "a decisive step in the process of a Jewish girl's Americanization."[25]

The store reached revenues of $6 million in 1887. But in the next decade, demand decreased, and the business relocated uptown to Broadway and Astor Place.

Sadly, what was once one of the most magnificent retail buildings in the world suffered severe fire damage in 1905. In 2012, a portion of the remaining parts of the building was granted landmark status. Today, you can still see the pink color of the building next to an upholstery shop and Chinese locksmith.

Seward Park
East Broadway to Grand Street, between Essex and Jefferson streets
Subway: F train to East Broadway

Seward Park is another example of an attempt by public officials,
philanthropists, and advocates for the poor to improve the lives of
the impoverished immigrants. In the late 1890s, social reformers
lobbied for public parks with recreational facilities to offer slum
dwellers an escape from stifling tenements. Lillian Wald, the
founder of the Henry Street Settlement, and Charles Stover, the
director of the University Settlement, established the Outdoor
Recreation League.[26] Between 1898 and 1902, the organization
opened nine privately sponsored playgrounds in municipal parks,
of which Seward Park was one.

The park was named after William H. Seward, United States
secretary of state in the mid-nineteenth century, who advocated
for immigrants, especially the Irish.

Today, the park is used by local Chinese residents. You may
notice t'ai chi practitioners exercising each morning.

Shtiebel/Shteeble Row
225–283 East Broadway

Shtiebel Row is a vestige of the dense immigrant population on
the Lower East Side. *Shtiebel,* Yiddish for "small room," refers to
a small synagogue. Unlike the grandiose synagogues of Temple
Emanu-El or Eldridge, these shuls were small and modest and
offered worshipers a simpler, more intimate atmosphere. The Lower
East Side was estimated to have between 350 and 500 synagogues
at its peak. Most were shtiebels. Some buildings housed 5 or 6,
many of them named after cities or villages in Eastern Europe
or perhaps originating from the *Landsmannschaft.* Others were
organized by trades such as shoemakers, plumbers, etc., giving
rise to nicknames such as "Tailor's Shul."

A few of these shuls still exist. There are several shtiebels along
East Broadway between Clinton and Montgomery streets, proof
that Jewish life thrives today as well as in the past. The following
is a list of some of them:

No. 223: Congregation Beth Hachasidim De Polen
No. 235: Agudas Harabonim: Ezras Torah Relief Society
No. 237: Congregation Shearis Adath Israel
No. 239: Congregation Austria Hungary Anshei Sfard
No. 241: Chevra Zemach Zedek
No. 247: Chevra Chassidei Boyaner
No. 249: Mizrachi Hapoel Hamizrachi

Former Schapiro's Kosher Winery Site
126 Rivington Street
Subway: J, M, or Z train to Delancey Street

Schapiro's Kosher Winery, like most businesses in the neighborhood, started as a simple store and restaurant on Attorney Street. An item on their menu would prove so popular it would ultimately propel their success. Customers raved about the honey wine—*mehd*—which was produced according to the traditional methods of kosher winemaking. Taking the cue from his customers, Sam Schapiro closed the restaurant and opened a winery on Rivington Street in 1899. Marketing increased the brand's popularity. In 1933, the jingle on the radio called it "wine so thick you can cut it with a knife."[27]

Today, the winery's headquarters is in Monticello, New York, with a store in the Essex Street Market. The Rivington Street store is closed, but its historic sign is visible.

Streit's Matzo Factory
150 Rivington Street (at Suffolk)
Admission: Free tours by appointment
Telephone: (212) 475-7000
Web site: www.streitsmatzos.com
Subway: F train to East Broadway

A factory in the middle of today's pricey Lower East Side would seem unlikely. Yet this one's continued presence reminds anyone walking by of the neighborhood's former days. The only remaining matzo factory in the area and the only one in America that is family owned and operated, Streit's Matzo factory produces traditional matzos for year-round consumption as well as specialty ones for Passover.

Peek in the window and catch a glimpse of workers making long sheets of matzos. Better yet, inquire about a tour of this unique facility.

Background

The story of this matzo factory begins in 1897 with Aron and Nettie Streit arriving from Austria. At 65 Pitt Street, the Streits made matzos in a humble bakery. The family business thrived, and soon production of matzos soared with increased demand and automated machinery.[28]

The business boomed in the densely packed Jewish neighborhood, and the budding company subsequently purchased several adjacent buildings. Descendants of the family now run the factory.

Over the years, many in the industry have been acquired by conglomerates. Streit's differentiates itself in the market by advertising that "while others have sold out to large corporations, we, at Streit's, continue our family tradition of bringing you the best matzos and kosher food products for Passover and year round."

Little has changed in the matzo-making business over the decades. According to Streit's, that is how consumers want it. They have perfected the production process to prevent leavening, which conforms not only to the requirements of Passover but also the year-round matzos: "Flour and water are mixed in giant vats, then rolled, flattened, and perforated by machine before being baked for 90 seconds at 900 degrees in one of 2 72-foot steel ovens. To prevent leavening, the process must take under 18 minutes. The baked matzos are moved into wire baskets along an overhead conveyer belt to cool before workers break them by hand into squares and pack them into boxes to be transported to warehouses for global distribution."[29]

Tip for the Visitor: Though it is not an official public tour, you may be able to schedule a factory tour by appointment. Call the office and inquire. Also, visit the shop, where you can purchase freshly baked matzos hot out of the oven.

United Jewish Council of the East Side
235 East Broadway
Telephone: (212) 233-6037
Web site: www.ujces.org
Subway: F train to East Broadway

Established in 1971 by community leaders and residents, the UJC provides various outreach programs for families, children, and senior citizens. The organization's mission is to "preserve and stabilize the Lower East Side of Manhattan community through the provision of a wide range of human services and community development programs."[30] Programs at various locations include social services, a kosher lunch club, a wheelchair-accessible passenger van, daily homecare services, mental-health facilities, and recreational and educational programs. The staff is multilingual, and funding is provided by the UJA-Federation of New York, various private and public foundations, and city and state agencies.

University Settlement House
184 Eldridge Street
Telephone: (212) 453-0242
Web site: www.universitysettlement.org
Subway: F train to East Broadway

Originally called the Neighborhood Guild and established in 1886, this settlement house pioneered the concept in the U.S. of living among the population one is serving. The idea was to bring in educated or elite men to "settle" the slums, not only to aid the impoverished immigrants but also serve as role models. At several previous locations, the Guild was a separated boys' and girls' club. In 1899, it relocated to its present home at 184 Eldridge Street.

Initial financial support came from industrialists such as Andrew Carnegie and John D. Rockefeller, but in 1891 universities took a more active role. That year, the president of Columbia University, Seth Low, encouraged his students and graduates to become volunteers. The settlement was more than a volunteer program, however. It served to mix social classes, as the idealistic, educated, and affluent worked with the underprivileged. Probably the most famous volunteer was the social reformer and future first lady Eleanor Roosevelt, who taught dance at the settlement. She worked with her fiancé, Franklin Delano Roosevelt, who saw poverty up close for the first time.

Today, the settlement continues to provide many needed social services and recreational activities for the new generation of residents, comprised primarily of Latinos and Chinese. Services target at-risk youth, young families, and senior citizens.[31] Although the demographics have changed, the organization still strives to offer hope and direction to those in need.

Visitor Center, Lower East Side Business Improvement District
54 Orchard Street
Open weekdays 9:30 a.m.–5:30 p.m., weekends 9:30 a.m.–4:00 p.m.
Admission: Free
Telephone: (212) 226-9010
Web site: www.lowereastsideny.com
Subway: F train to Second Avenue

Inquire at the Lower East Side Business Improvement District (LES BID) about events such as fashion shows and food festivals like the famed International Pickle Day festival and New York City Apple Day. Also check out any walking tours of historical sites or art galleries.

The Visitor Center offers free Wi-Fi, and staff can offer tips on sightseeing, shopping, and nightlife.[32]

Williamsburg Bridge
Eastern End of Delancey Street

Constructed in 1903, this bridge, and the trolley service that followed, caused a shift in Lower East Side workers' lives. With its completion, they began to move to more spacious Brooklyn and commute to Manhattan. The pedestrian walkway allowed Orthodox Shabbat observers residing in Brooklyn to attend their synagogues on the Lower East Side. The media nicknamed the bridge the "Jews' Highway."[33]

After World War II, Satmar Hasidic Jews settled in Williamsburg at the Brooklyn end of the bridge, living among working-class Latinos. Development of the neighborhood followed the typical pattern for New York. Artists seeking cheap rent moved into lofts and provided more cultural alternatives.[34] When New York's real-estate market boomed in the mid-1990s, many tenants were priced out of Manhattan, demand skyrocketed in Williamsburg, and gentrification ensued. Soon afterward, developers seized on this trend and began building luxury condos in the formerly industrial and multiethnic neighborhood.[35]

Historic Synagogues

Angel Orensanz Foundation Center for the Arts
172 Norfolk Street
Telephone: (212) 529-7194
Web site: www.orensanz.org
Subway: J, M, or Z train to Essex Street

The building's striking Gothic Revival design, with pointed archways in pink and gray, is a reminder of its synagogue past. Currently an arts center, the Angel Orensanz Foundation Center for the Arts was built in 1849 and is "the oldest surviving structure in the city built specifically as a synagogue."

Try to enter the onetime synagogue and observe its majestic sanctuary. Observe the striking blue and pink translucent lighting. Look for clues of its synagogue past in the faded rose window and the mini-balconies on the side. Also be sure to visit the art gallery on the upper floors.

Background

Congregation Anshe Chesed purchased the three lots upon which the synagogue was built for $10,500 ($293,000 today).[36] As a historic irony, the lots were part of Peter Stuyvesant's estate. He had tried to turn away the first Jews who arrived in New Amsterdam in 1654.

At the time of its completion, it was the largest synagogue building in America, with a sanctuary for 1,200. Founded in 1828, Anshe Chesed was the third Jewish congregation in New York, after Shearith Israel (1655) and B'nai Jeshurun (1825). Congregants were German, Dutch, and Polish Jews. It served as New York's second Reform temple in 1850; Congregation Emanu-El was established in 1845. As part of its Reform ritual, the pulpit faced the congregation, music was part of the service (which is prohibited on the Sabbath in Orthodox synagogues), and services were led in German or English rather than Hebrew.[37]

Following the pattern of similar congregations, Anshe Chesed relocated uptown in 1874 and merged with Adas Jeshurun to form Temple Beth El. That congregation became part of Congregation Emanu-El in 1927. The building was then utilized by Orthodox congregations Shaarey Rachamim, Oheb Zedek, and Anche Slonim from 1921 until 1974—all of which were established by Eastern European Jews. Originally built for Reform services, the sanctuary was altered to suit Orthodox services. The organ was removed, the pulpit was turned toward the east, and services were conducted only in Hebrew.

Abandoned in 1974, the dilapidated structure was a byproduct of a neighborhood in decline. The historic synagogue's fate changed in 1986 when Angel Orensanz, an internationally renowned Spanish painter and sculptor, discovered the decaying building while exploring the neighborhood in search of a studio space for his sculpture. Orensanz was intrigued by the light filtering through the broken windows and the contemplative atmosphere of the vertical space. He purchased the building for $500,000 ($1,060,000 today). He then transformed it into an arts center, currently used for theatrical performances, gallery shows, film festivals, photo shoots, weddings, and fundraisers.

In 1999, a small congregation known as the Shul of New York began worshiping in the basement study hall. Though its weekly services are now held elsewhere, it still uses the space for High Holy Day services. Coincidentally, the congregation acquired a Torah that turned out to come from Slonim in Belarus, Poland, the hometown of the last congregation to occupy this building.[38]

Architecture of Angel Orensanz Center

The building's Gothic Revival style borrowed from two German churches: Cologne Cathedral and Friedrichswerder Church in Berlin. Dominating the façade are pointed-arch windows and doorways. It is also said that "the building's interior resembles that of the Cathedral of Notre-Dame in Paris and the sanctuary was designed to resemble the Sistine Chapel."[39]

Former Beth Hamedrash Hagadol ("House of Study")
60 Norfolk Street
Subway: F train to East Broadway

This former church turned synagogue sits idly on Norfolk Street. Once a bustling house of worship, it has not been in use for several years. Sadly, it stands as a symbol of decay, with overgrown branches and a dilapidated interior. At present, it is closed, having been judged unsafe to enter.

The historic building has landmark status. It was one of the first New York City synagogues to receive this honor and the first in Lower Manhattan. The Lower East Side Jewish Conservancy raised funds for a restoration feasibility study and urgent repairs and launched a major initiative for additional monies for interior structural stabilization.

In 2013, however, the synagogue applied for hardship status to allow demolition of the building and the construction of condos in its place. This application was then withdrawn. However, given the building's structural decay and financial unsoundness, its future remains uncertain.

Background

Built as the Norfolk Street Baptist Church, this mid-nineteenth-century Gothic Revival structure was later home to a Methodist congregation. As the neighborhood transitioned from a predominantly German and Christian one to a more Jewish one during the 1880s, the building's function changed once again.

In 1885, Beth Hamedrash Hagadol ("House of Study") acquired the building and remodeled it into a synagogue. The congregation was the "first Russian Jewish congregation in America, and the first Eastern European congregation in New York City."[40] The congregation was founded in an attic on Bayard Street by those rejecting the growing Reform movement. Other locations for the budding congregation included the infamous "Five Points," a neighborhood known for its gangs, crime, and poverty; Allen Street in the Lower East Side; Grand and Forsyth streets; a former courthouse on Clinton Street; and then Ludlow Street, where the congregation purchased its first synagogue building. Finally, in 1885, the congregation bought the Norfolk Street Baptist Church.[41]

According to Jeffrey Gurock's *The History of Judaism in America*, Beth Hamedrash Hagadol "provided an atmosphere that was socially religious," in which Jews would "combine piety with pleasure." He continued, "They want[ed] everyone present to join and chant the prayers; above all they scorn[ed] a regularly ordained cantor. In contrast to the informality of the services, members scrupulously observed the Jewish dietary laws, and every member personally oversaw the baking of his matzos for use on Passover."[42]

Bialystoker Synagogue (Orthodox)
7 Bialystoker Place
Admission: Call Hondo Abramowitz between 7 and 10 a.m. to arrange a tour. Check the Web site for current information.
Telephone: (212) 475-0165
Web site: www.bialystoker.org
Subway: F train to East Broadway

The refurbished Bialystoker Synagogue is among the most beautiful in New York. If you are interested in historic synagogues,

Formerly a Methodist Episcopal church constructed in 1826, the sanctuary is one of the most magnificent in the Lower East Side. (Photograph by Jessica Siemens.)

this is a must-see. The understated gray, three-door exterior belies its magnificent interior. To see the inside, go on a tour or, if appropriate, attend services. Observers will marvel at the ornamented floral design of the sanctuary, intricate woodcarvings, and lush wall and ceiling murals. Pear-shaped, crystal chandeliers hang from Stars of David on the ceiling.

The sanctuary does not face Jerusalem, so a mural of the Western Wall appears on the eastern side. Symbols are arranged throughout the bright and colorful ceiling. Each one represents a holiday or ritual. For example, two tablets symbolizing the Ten Commandments signify the holiday of Shavout, which commemorates Moses's reception of the Torah on Mount Sinai. The pews in the front are from the building's church days.

Background

The building was erected in 1826 as the Willett Street Methodist Episcopal Church, catering to the large German population in the area that was known at the time as *Klein Deutschland* or "Little Germany." The Bialystoker Synagogue was purchased in 1905 by an Orthodox congregation founded in 1865 as Chevra Anshei Chesed, by Jews from Bialystok in eastern Poland. This followed the tradition of immigrants from the same town forming communities and places of worship within their larger neighborhoods. Often these congregations moved several times throughout the city. The Bialystok congregation was no exception. Housed in a Hester Street building, the budding congregation later transferred to Orchard Street and finally to this location.

Twenty-five years after this purchase, during the Great Depression, the congregation decided to improve the main sanctuary in order to inspire the community. It was modeled after the Bialystok Synagogue in Eastern Europe. In 1988, the synagogue renovated the marvelous sanctuary.

Architecture of the Bialystoker

New York City historian Gerard Wolfe notes in his 2013 book *The Synagogues of New York's Lower East Side* that the Bialystoker Synagogue is one of the "most exuberant examples of synagogue decoration in the metropolitan New York area."

A clue to the building's fascinating past lies in the women's gallery. In a rear corner, there is a hidden door through which a ladder leads to the attic. Some historians believe that this was a station on the Underground Railroad where runaway slaves hid until they could be transported to Canada. Wolfe points out that members of the "Methodist Church were often Abolitionists, lending credibility to the oral traditions of the secret hideaway."[43]

The congregation is still vibrant today. Perhaps its most famous member is Sheldon Silver, the famed Democratic speaker of the New York State Assembly. The son of Russian immigrants, he was born on the Lower East Side in 1944 and first elected to the Assembly in 1976.

Congregation Chasam Sopher (Orthodox)

8 Clinton Street
Telephone: (212) 777-5140
Web site: www.chasamsopher.org
Subway: F train to Second Avenue

Round arches accentuate this handsome brick building. A tranquil garden lies to the right, with a historic streetlamp hanging in front. The second-oldest synagogue building in New York, Chasam Sopher is surely worth a visit.

Background

In 1853, Rodeph Sholom, a congregation of German Jewish immigrants worshiping at 187 Attorney Street, erected this building. Thus, it was constructed as a synagogue, unlike the Bialystoker and Sixth Street synagogues, among others, which were converted from former churches.

Though it began as an Orthodox congregation, it gradually adopted Reform practices. The rabbi, Aaron Wise, was the father of the famous Rabbi Stephen Wise, a leader of the Reform movement and prominent Zionist. Signs of the Reform adoption included a choir, organ, and English-language sermons. Rodeph Sholom left the neighborhood in 1891 for a new synagogue on the growing Upper East Side at Sixty-Third and Lexington, then relocated to its current building on West Eighty-Third Street between Columbus Avenue and Central Park West. The congregation predates the building. In 1842, it was founded as a society to care for the sick and needy who worshiped on Attorney Street until the 1853 construction of the synagogue.

In 1887, the red-brick synagogue was engulfed by a fire. The building subsequently underwent major repairs and restoration. Four years later, its occupancy changed hands. When Rodeph Sholom moved out, Congregation Chasam Sopher replaced it. The newly formed congregation resulted from the union of two Polish societies named for their hometowns of Czestochowa and Unterstanestier. "Chasam Sopher" is a reference to the German rabbi Moshe Schreiber.[44]

The once-thriving synagogue suffered a decline as the neighborhood saw an economic downturn coupled with plummeting numbers of aging Jews in the area. Funds and members became scarce. Unfortunately, many synagogues shut their doors forever.[45]

But this synagogue has a comeback story. It is an example of highly successful conservation, thanks in large part to Moshe Weiser. A pioneer during the downturn, he asked the press for help when the historic building was about to shut its doors. The building was thoroughly refurbished and rededicated in 2006.[46]

Eldridge Street Synagogue (Orthodox)

12 Eldridge Street (between Canal and Division)
Telephone: (212) 219-0888
Web site: www.eldridgestreet.org
Subway: F train to East Broadway; or B or D to Grand Street; or 6, N, R, Q, J, or Z to Canal Street

See the "Museums" section above for information on both the Eldridge Street Synagogue and the separately managed Museum at Eldridge Street.

Site of Congregation Emanu-El

409 Grand Street
Subway: F train to East Broadway

The outgrowth of *Culturs Verein*, or "Cultural Society," formed by German Jews in 1845, Temple Emanu-El was the premier Reform congregation in New York and the third most prominent in the nation.[46] During its first three years, services were conducted in rented rooms on the second floor of the building that once stood at this site, on the southeast corner of Grand and Clinton.[47] The congregation's rituals were a mixture of Reform and traditional. For example, it formed a choir, a practice generally not found in Orthodox congregations. Yet, in keeping with traditions, men wore head coverings and prayer shawls and were seated in the front rows, while women sat in the rear.

   In 1848, Emanu-El acquired a former Methodist church at 56 Chrystie Street, between Hester and Canal. The congregation introduced some additional Reform elements. It added an organ and adopted drastic changes in liturgy and ritual. In 1854, the growing congregation relocated to 120 East Twelfth Street, taking over a Baptist church in the northern part of the predominantly German neighborhood. The congregation took on additional Reform elements in its new location.

   Fourteen years later, the congregation constructed its own

Restored interior of Eldridge Street Synagogue. Photograph by Kate Milford.
(Courtesy Museum at Eldridge Street)

synagogue building on the corner of Fifth Avenue and Forty-Third Street, in what was then a trendy residential neighborhood. In 1927, Emanu-El merged with Beth-El and moved to the site of the Astor family mansion at Fifth Avenue and Sixty-Fifth Street, its current location. (See the synagogues section in the Upper East Side chapter for more information.)

Former First Roumanian-American Synagogue
70 Hester Street

In 1860, a group of Romanian immigrants established the First Roumanian-American Congregation, also referred to as Congregation Shaarey Shomayim ("Gates of Heaven"). Occupying this site from 1894 to 1904, it then relocated to Rivington Street, where it remained until that building was demolished in 2006. The three-story brick Hester Street building has been converted into apartments and commercial space, but you can still observe the Moorish-style windows on the upper floors.

Rivington Street Site, First Roumanian-American Congregation
Rivington Street, just east of Orchard Street

Today, the site of the Rivington Street building that housed the First Roumanian-American Congregation stands vacant. It is one of the few lots in the neighborhood that has no building. The recent history of this congregation is a cautionary tale of building negligence. At the end of the twentieth century, the building was badly in need of repair, but the congregation was reported to have rejected financial assistance for renovations. In December 2005, water damage was found. A few months later, the roof caved in, and the building was soon demolished. According to one eyewitness, "It sounded like an explosion, then a loud crash."[48] The city and the congregation point fingers at each other for forcing the demolition.

"If nothing else, the wreckage on Rivington Street provides a cautionary tale," Peg Breen, president of the New York Landmarks Conservancy, told the *New York Times*. "People don't come out of rabbinical school or seminary with a lot of course work in building maintenance. It is a shame there are not more sources of funding to help."[49]

Background
Reflecting the largely German Protestant neighborhood, the Rivington Street building was constructed as a Protestant church circa 1860 by the Second Reformed Presbyterian Church congregation. Like other churches, it was sold to a Jewish congregation as German Protestants left the neighborhood. The

buyer was Congregation Shaarey Shomayim, a German Orthodox congregation that began in 1841. They remodeled the building, but as the size of their congregation declined, they sold it. Around 1902, the First Roumanian-American Congregation bought it.

In its new space on Rivington Street, the synagogue became known as the "Cantor's Carnegie Hall" because of its theatrical-like acoustics and seating capacity. It was no stranger to fame. During a period when synagogues were competing for renowned cantors, the most acclaimed cantor of the time, Yossele Rosenblatt, sang there.

The congregation declined to double digits by the 2000s, driven by a decrease in Jews living within walking in distance of the synagogue, a requirement for Orthodox Jews to attend services.

Congregation Kehila Kedosha Janina (Holy Community of Janina)

280 Broome Street (at Allen Street)
Museum open daily 11 a.m.–4 p.m., tours Sunday 11 a.m.–3 p.m.
Admission: Donation
Telephone: (212) 431-1619
Web site: www.kkjsm.org
Subway: F, J, or M train to Delancey
Affiliation: Greek Sephardic Romaniote

Departing from the more typical Eastern European historical synagogues prevalent in this neighborhood, Kehila Kedosha Janina was formed in 1906 by a group of Jews from Janina in northwest Greece. Built in 1927, the narrow, two-story, buff-colored brick building embellishes the drab storefronts and apartment façades on the block. Janina is the sole Greek synagogue in the area and, remarkably, one of the only remaining synagogues with roots stretching back to Roman times. According to tradition, Romaniotes were Jews who were exiled to Rome on slave ships after Romans destroyed the Second Temple in Jerusalem. The story alleges that a "storm forced them to land in Greece where they developed local customs over the following two millennia."[50] The word *Romaniote* is actually a Hellenized Latin term for "Greece" or "second Rome."

Interior of the only Romaniote synagogue in the Western Hemisphere

Unlike the Ashkenazi synagogues that dominate the area, Janina follows a Greek Sephardic tradition, with its own liturgical compositions accompanied by Greek chants. Quintessentially Sephardic, the reader's platform, or *bimah*, faces the Ark from the center of the synagogue. The seating arrangement echoed that of the synagogue in Ioannina, a town in northwest Greece. According to Romaniote custom, the women's section took up three sides of the balcony.

The growing congregation stumbled after World War II as many families moved to the more spacious uptown and outlying areas of the city. During the 1950s, membership decreased, and the congregation could no longer afford a rabbi. For four decades, Hy Genee ran the synagogue. He died in 2006.

Museum Director Marcia Haddad Ikonomopoulos describes the uniqueness of the synagogue and explains its survival:

When we opened our doors in 1927, we were one of over four hundred Jewish houses of worship south of Houston Street on the Lower East Side. We, now, are one of only five that date from the 1920s. It is my personal belief that this is due to two things; first, this community was "outside the box," to use a modern term. There was no other synagogue with which they could merge. Second, and most importantly, this community was comfortable in their own shoes. They loved who they were and were passionate about their special "Greekness." They passed this passion and perseverance on to subsequent generations.

Today, the congregation is enjoying a revival of sorts. Though only a few Romaniote Jews remain on the Lower East Side, the synagogue maintains a sizeable mailing list. As the neighborhood rejuvenates and young people move back to the area—often looking for ways to connect to their ancestral past— participation in traditional ceremonies at the synagogue has increased. Several congregants are currently collaborating on a project to document the lives of earlier generations of Greek Jews through census records, ships' manifests, and related archives.

The synagogue also contains a museum of Greek Jewish history, which occupies the former women's balcony. Ikonomopoulos notes its significance. "We are the only Romaniote synagogue in the Western Hemisphere. Through our synagogue and museum we preserve not only the liturgy of Greek-speaking Jews but, also, the customs and traditions." On display are maps, photographs, and artifacts detailing the customs of Romaniote Jews. The museum tells the little-known story of Jewish communities in Greece and their fate under Nazi rule. Greek Jews suffered disproportionately during the Holocaust. Visitors are encouraged to discover the differences between the Romaniote and the Sephardic traditions. Objects on exhibit include a traditional Turkish dress and a nineteenth-century wedding dress. The museum includes a small literary center, art gallery, and bookshop.

For more information, view the documentary *The Last Greeks on Broome Street*. It is directed, written, and narrated by the great-grandson of the founders of this unique congregation. The congregation organizes an annual tour to Jewish Greece sponsored by the Association of Friends of Greek Jewry.

Tip for the Visitor: Inquire about a personal tour coupled with a Jewish-Greek meal with the museum's director. Also, check out the book/gift shop on the second floor, which has the world's largest selection of books in English about the Jews of Greece.

Former Pike Street Shul
15 Pike Street
Subway: F train to East Broadway

One of the Lower East Side's great historic synagogues, the Pike Street Shul embodies the rise, fall, and renewal of its neighborhood. The synagogue was founded by Polish and Russian Jews who broke away from their congregation. It was originally called Beth Hamedrash Livne Yisroel Yelide Polen ("House of Study of the Children of Israel Born in Poland"), and after a merger, its name was changed to Sons of Israel Kalwarie. It is best known for its Isaac Elchanan Theological Seminary, which taught students in the ladies' gallery. After merging with another seminary in 1915, it moved to Washington Heights in 1928 and became the renowned Yeshiva University. The synagogue was one of the wealthiest on the Lower East Side and gave birth to the Young Israel Movement.

As the congregation dwindled, several members decided to sell the building to a local Chinese church. But they never asked permission from the other members, who were living out of state. After several years of litigation, a judge allowed the sale. During this time, the building was neglected, And vandals stole valuable items.

Today, it is a designated New York City landmark and functions as a mixed-use building with commercial space on the ground floor, a Buddhist temple in a part of what was the sanctuary, and apartments on the upper floors. The exterior of the building is still impressive. The four-story, limestone structure was influenced by German architecture. Its façade consists of a central section with a double lateral staircase that leads up one story to the main entrance. New additions for the Buddhist temple include two large, Asian stone lions at the front entrance and a huge incense burner near the center of the main floor.

Stanton Street Shul (Orthodox)

180 Stanton Street (between Clinton and Anthony)
Web site: www.stantonstshul.com
Subway: J, M, or Z train to Essex; or F to Delancey

The Stanton Street Shul's tenement structure blends in seamlessly with the surrounding buildings. One of the few remaining tenement-style synagogues, its resurging membership is a testament to urban renewal.

Background

Organized by a group from Galicia, Poland in 1913 as Congregation B'nai Jacob Anshe Brzezan, the Stanton Street Synagogue is a tenement-style shul with a sanctuary measuring 20 feet wide by 100 feet long and was designed to accommodate 400 worshipers. It was converted from a three-story, wood-frame front house and a brick rear house in 1913 for $10,000. Essentially, two tenements were combined.

The building's layout is similar to those built around the same time. The neoclassical brick façade is distinguished by four two-story cast stone pilasters supporting an entablature and a pediment, inscribed in Hebrew with the name of the shul. Inside, you will see Zodiac signs representing different months. The Bialystok shul and this one are the only remaining synagogues in the area with these symbols on their walls.

Similar to other synagogues on the Lower East Side, its congregation diminished in the 1950s. To stem the decline, in 1952 Congregation B'nai Jacob Anshe Brzezan (the formal name for the Stanton Shul) joined Congregation Bnai Joseph Dugel

Macheneh Ephraim. The shul survived dramatic economic and cultural changes in the neighborhood.

For several decades, this tenement-style shul suffered decay. In 2002, it was rescued from a proposed sale to a Jesuit theater group. Rabbi Joseph Singer sustained the congregation from the 1960s to the 1990s. To catch a glimpse of what the synagogue looked like in the late 1970s, view the 1979 film *Last Embrace*, directed by Jonathan Demme and based on the novel *The 13th Man*. The film has both interior and exterior shots of the shul.

The shul has also been reinvigorated in recent years by a new group of Jews moving into the neighborhood. The congregation blends groups such as the old-timers of the area and younger singles and couples.

Today, the congregation is raising funds to refurbish the aging building. Volunteers have been repairing serious water damage. Renovation of the basement worship area was completed in 2007, turning a dark, tunnel-like room into a multifunctional space.

According to Elissa Sampson, a Stanton Street Shul board member, "If someone wanted a really gorgeous suburban synagogue, they wouldn't be coming here. What they get is something homelike, something real and familiar . . . a piece of the Old Country."

Eateries

Doughnut Plant
Telephone: (212) 505-3700
Web site: www.doughnutplant.com
Prices: Inexpensive
Subway: F train to East Broadway

Do you know the difference between cake and yeast doughnuts? Have you tried a "blackout" doughnut?

Known for selling delicious doughnuts, Doughnut Plant offers both "cake" and "yeast." Flavors are novel and include the popular "blackout," *crème brûlée*, strawberry, pistachio, *tres leches*, peanut-butter glaze, and Valrhona chocolate.

Background

The shop's creator, Mark Israel, is a third-generation baker. His grandfather served with the U.S. Army in Bakery Company 351 in Paris during World War I and afterward owned a bakery in North Carolina, which was later run by Mark's father.[51]

In 1994, the family tradition continued. Mark began making doughnuts by hand from his grandfather's recipe but with a twist. He added organic glazes and delivered the goodies to gourmet food markets and cafés. In 2000, he opened a small shop at this location. In the early 2000s, he partnered with a businessman in Japan and opened nine bakeries in Tokyo and one in Seoul. In 2012, he expanded the current location to accommodate a growing number of customers.

Economy Candy
108 Rivington (between Essex and Ludlow)
Telephone: (212) 254-1531
Web site: www.economycandy.com
Prices: Depend on specialty of item
Subway: F train to Delancey

The phrase "kid in a candy store" comes to life at Economy Candy. No matter what your generation, you will recognize candy brands you probably have not seen in years. Rediscover—or discover for the first time—jujubes, chocolate-covered graham crackers, Good n' Plenty, original Bazookas, Big League Chews, and wax fangs. Or explore new kinds of candy, chocolate, or nuts. Go back in time to when corner candy stores were more common.

Started in 1937 by the Greek Jewish Cohen family, Economy Candy is a family-owned candy store harkening back to simpler times. For older visitors, it may be nostalgic. The "Nosher's Paradise of the Lower East Side," the store stocks enduring favorites: Sugar Daddies, Tootsie Pops, rock candy in colors such as orange and purple, gumballs, Atomic Fireballs, Gummi Bears, Fruit Slices, and more.[52]

The first store, located on the northeast corner of Essex and Rivington, sold candy, nuts, and dried fruits inside and piled high on carts on the sidewalk. After World War II, Moish Cohen took over the store from one of his uncles. In 1985, the business moved to its current location and added items such as coffee, tea, jam, and spices. The store is currently run by Moish's son, Jerry Cohen, and his family.

Katz's Deli
205 East Houston Street (at Ludlow)
Telephone: (212) 254-2246
Web site: www.katzsdelicatessen.com
Prices: Moderate

Katz's is the centerpiece of Lower East Side culinary history. It parallels the history of the neighborhood, from its founding by immigrants to serving Yiddish theater patrons, its service during World War II, and its later years in pop culture. The iconic deli is best known for its turkey, pastrami, and corned beef.

The deli's name changed during its earlier years from Iceland Brothers to Iceland & Katz, after Willy Katz bought into the concern. The establishment's current name came about when Katz's cousin Benny entered the business in 1910.

The original location was across the street until the expanding subway required merchants to move their businesses—a fact of life in the city that continues to this day, with the building of the Second Avenue subway as the current example. Unlike the packed storefronts of later years, the lot on Houston Street in front of the popular deli had barrels of meat and pickles until the late 1940s.

During World War II, the store's slogan was born: "Send a Salami to Your Boy in the Army." Historically, families sent care packages to their sons fighting overseas.

After Benny Katz and Harry Tarowsky died in the late 1970s, their descendants ran the deli. Partners took over in subsequent years. To this day the deli keeps many of its traditions. The famous slogan continues to be relevant as customers send delicacies to American soldiers in Afghanistan. Updates are visible as well, with walls that once showcased pictures of famous Yiddish actors now displaying current celebrities and heads of state.

Payment by a ticket is still used. Orders are written on the tickets, and customers surrender them as they exit the restaurant.

Katz's Delicatessen, founded in 1888, still uses a unique ticket system for billing customers. (Photograph by Jessica Siemens.)

Katz's has been the site of multiple pop-culture moments. The 1989 comedy *When Harry Met Sally* features the fake orgasm scene in the restaurant, with the quote, "I'll have what she's having."[53]

The restaurant offers customers a choice of self-service with seating on one side of the room or waiter service on the other side. Go discover what the fuss is about at Katz's Deli—but remember to hold on to your ticket!

Kossar's Bialys (Kosher)

367 Grand Street (at Clinton Street)
Closed Saturday
Telephone: (212) 473-4810
Web site: www.kossarsbialys.com
Prices: Inexpensive
Subway: J, M, or Z train to Essex; or F to Delancey

Have you tried a bialy? Do you know what one is? A "cousin to the bagel," the bialy is a soft, crusty yeast roll topped with browned onions, handmade and typically baked in an old brick oven. The nation's oldest bialy shop, Kossar's Bialys, has been baking bialys and associated products since the 1950s. The bakery produces about eight hundred dozen weekly (actually six days since they are closed on Saturday), selling both retail and wholesale to premium outlets such as Zabar's and Fairway.

The process of making bialys is simple yet labor intensive. Gluten flour is added to freshly ground onions and baked in an old-fashioned brick oven. There is a beauty standard for the bialy. The "ideal Bialy has a full-looking round shape around the outer rim and a defined indentation in the center with fresh onions patted into the middle."[54]

Mimi Sheraton, author of *The Bialy Eaters*, published in 2000, apprenticed in the art of bialy baking at Kossar's. The book recounts her travels in 1994 to Bialystok, Poland, the town for which the bialy is named.

Pickle Guys (Kosher)
49 Essex Street (between Grand and Hester)
Closed Saturday
Telephone: (212) 656-9739
Web site: www.pickleguys.com
Prices: Inexpensive

Though once a staple on the Lower East Side, just one barrel pickle seller remains in the neighborhood: Pickle Guys. Explore the variety of pickle flavors and their degrees of sourness. Also try the many kinds of pickled tomatoes, olives, and sundried tomatoes.

Alan Kaufman, a seasoned pickler, is the owner. He is the former manager of the famed Guss' pickles, a neighborhood institution that moved to Brooklyn in 2009. Kaufman explains that he makes pickles the way his mother did, from an old Eastern European recipe. "The pickles are made by letting them sit in salt brine with garlic, spices, and no preservatives. Storing them in barrels, from a day up to six months, the pickles cure as they sit."[55]

Russ and Daughters
179 East Houston Street
Telephone: (212) 475-4880
Web site: www.russanddaughters.com
Prices: Moderate
Subway: F train to Second Avenue; or F, J, M or Z to Delancey
    Street

Russ and Daughters is a must stop on the Lower East Side culinary tour. Opened in 1914, this landmark institution is famous for its candy, chocolates, caviar, smoked fish, and herring. Be sure to sample the smoked fish from around the world.

Background
The store's humble origins mirrored those of many immigrants scraping out a living and hoping to have a pushcart—and one day, their own store. The story begins with Joel Russ, an Eastern European immigrant who sold Polish mushrooms until he could

purchase a pushcart and add items such as pickled herring. In 1914, he transitioned to a storefront, opening Russ International Appetizers around the corner from the current location. Six years later, he moved to the current location, and in 1933 he renamed the business Russ and Daughters after making his three daughters partners. This deviated from the tradition of including sons in the family business, but Russ only had daughters. Thus, the move was recognized as more practically than socially motivated. Mark Federman, the current owner, wrote a book entitled *Russ and Daughters: Reflections and Recipes from the House the Herring Built* that outlined the history of the storied institution.

In 2013, National Public Radio ran a segment on the iconic store called "Family Keeps Jewish Soul Food Alive." On the program, Federman recounted, "The daughters Hattie, Ida, and Anne helped the business in other ways. . . . These pretty young girls would be fishing herrings out of barrels and slicing lox and charming and disarming the toughest of New York's customers. And these were tough customers."[56]

Shalom Chai (Kosher)
359 Grand Street (at Clinton)
Closed Saturday
Telephone: (212) 598-4178
Prices: Moderate
Subway: J, M, or Z train to Essex; or F to Delancey

Shalom Chai is a kosher dairy cafeteria featuring pizza and calzones along with hummus and bagels. It also has pasta and other Italian-style dishes.

Yonah Shimmel Knish Bakery
137 East Houston Street
Telephone: (212) 477-2858
Web site: www.knishery.com
Prices: Moderate
Subway: F train to Second Avenue (at Forsyth Street)

The décor harkens back to another era and is reason enough to

Yonah Shimmel Knish Bakery, founded in 1910 by a Romanian rabbi, is one of the oldest surviving knisheries in the nation. (Photograph by Jessica Siemens)

visit. The unique institution can seem more like a time capsule or museum than a restaurant. Walls are lined with photographs and newspaper clippings dating back to the early twentieth century. Pop culture has taken notice. It is featured in the 2009 film *Whatever Works,* with Larry David and Woody Allen.

The bakery offers both takeout and sit-down service, with a vast array of sweet or savory stuffings in the knishes, including cherry cheese, blueberry cheese, chocolate, broccoli, mushroom, sweet potato, and mixed vegetable. A new item on the menu is the barbeque knish. Diners eating in can also order iconic drinks once popular in the neighborhood, such as lime rickeys and egg creams, as well as classic Eastern European foods such as noodle kugel, chicken noodle and split pea soups, and borscht.

New flavors are being added to appeal to contemporary tastes. More than a century old, the bakery caters to various customers: "the traditional knish lovers who grew up on them; tourists who don't know what a knish is; and a newer, younger generation that may not necessarily have had knishes before or know they are supposed to be eaten with a dollop of mustard."[57] The Lower East Side continues to change. As gentrification expands, luxury condos, fashionable restaurants, and trendy hotels stand where timeworn storefronts once did. But Yonah Shimmel's still stands, seemingly unchanged barring the occasional menu enhancements.

Background

Yonah Shimmel was a Romanian rabbi who, like many immigrants on the Lower East Side, needed to supplement his income. Catering to the tastes of Eastern European immigrants, he used a pushcart to sell knishes in 1890. He moved up to a retail store on Houston Street that he rented with his cousin, Joseph Berger. The store relocated in 1910, as did many nearby businesses at the time, and landed at its current site. More than a century later, it is one of the few knisheries in the United States.

What Are Knishes?: One definition is a "thin dough shell filled with potato or buckwheat groats (kasha) and finely chopped onion, but the ingredients run the gamut from spinach to blueberry cheese to a variety of vegetables or kasha."[58] Food historians debate their origins. Knishes also have served as important props for New York politicians. Most elected officials over the decades have at least one photo op with a knish at some point during their campaign.[59]

Greenwich Village and East Village

Stroll through the Jewish Rialto, the stretch of Second Avenue that was home to two dozen Yiddish theaters during the late nineteenth and early twentieth centuries. Trace the history of these theaters that later became famous music venues, film houses, and off-Broadway stages. Catch a concert at the Hebrew Union College. Visit the site of the tragic Triangle Shirtwaist Factory fire.

The Jewish Rialto (Yiddish Theater District)

Second Avenue was "Broadway" for Yiddish theater from the late nineteenth century until just before World War II. "Between 1890 and 1940, there were more than 200 Yiddish theaters or touring Yiddish theater troupes in the United States, primarily in New York on Second Avenue, in the current East Village," states a historical survey of theaters in New York. "The neighborhood was known as *the Jewish Rialto.* At the time the U.S. entered World War I, there were 22 Yiddish theaters and two Yiddish vaudeville houses in New York City."[1]

While visiting the former Yiddish theaters, you need to use your imagination. Many are now apartment buildings, movie houses, banks, supermarkets, or off-Broadway theaters. Yet you can still detect their Yiddish past in their architecture, Jewish symbols, or Hebrew lettering. Some buildings even display photos of their history for public viewing.

Background

"Yiddish theater" designates plays performed in Yiddish. Some plays comprised original stories, others were derived from classic plays, while still others depicted key literature-centered Jewish

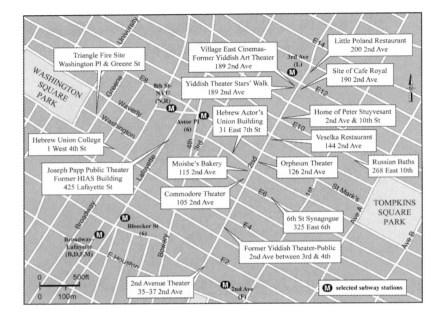

holidays, such as Purim (the Book of Esther). Many of the early plots were highly sentimental and portrayed the characters' longing for the Old Country. They featured tales of life in the shtetls (small Jewish villages in Central and Eastern Europe) and included music, song, and dance. Immigrant audiences could easily identify with the characters, plots, and settings.

Like the broader entertainment world, Yiddish theater also presented commercial, mass-oriented plays, with varying levels of success. Educational productions often had less appeal. Many of these playwrights wanted to use theater for a higher purpose—not only to amuse but to inspire or even transform their audiences. Playwright Jacob Gordin was an example. He stated that his aim was "rather than to pander to the public's taste for cheap *shund* [trash] plays to secure goodwill of the East Side's intelligentsia with literature," according to the historical survey. "These playwrights increasingly incorporated the concepts of true art and serious drama into their public image."[2]

The press was generally favorable toward the genre. In 1908, the *New York Times* wrote, "The dense Jewish population on the

Lower East Side of Manhattan shows in its appreciation of its own humble Yiddish poetry and the drama much the same spirit that controlled the rough audiences of the Elizabethan theater. There, as in the London of the sixteenth century, is a veritable intellectual renascence."

In later years, the press noted the transformation of the genre. A 1925 *New York Times* article asserted, "The Yiddish theater has been thoroughly Americanized . . . it is now a stable American institution and no longer dependent on immigration from Eastern Europe. Those who can neither speak nor write Yiddish attend Yiddish stage performances and pay Broadway prices on Second Avenue. This is attributed to the fact that Yiddish theater is in full flower."

In the early twentieth century, when Yiddish theater was becoming more established, some of its actors crossed over to Broadway. The prime example is Jacob Adler's portrayal of Shylock in a 1903 production of *The Merchant of Venice*. Molly Picon was another performer who crossed over from prime Yiddish-language roles to English-language theater.

According to Herb Latner, a child actor in the Yiddish theater, the professional Yiddish theatrical groups enjoyed prominent runs from the late 1880s until the 1940s, and over that time the quality of their productions improved. But beginning in the 1950s, the number of theaters started to diminish, and in the 1960s and '70s there was a dramatic decline. From the 1980s until the present, the only active Yiddish theater has been the Folksbiene. In some ways this is ironic, because in the past it was considered a more amateurish, less commercially established body. It is the sole survivor primarily due to support by Jewish organizations. A recent book called *Stardust Lost* (2006) details the history of the theater in a compelling way.

Today, there are four institutions associated with Yiddish theater in the U.S.:

- Folksbiene (National Yiddish Theatre). Produced primarily at Baruch College (in Manhattan), this troupe performs in Yiddish but has translations in English and Russian. It attempts to bring in younger audiences.
- Milken Archive of American Jewish Music. This institution

(in Santa Monica, California) seeks to conserve Jewish music, including Yiddish music.

- Yiddish Artists and Friends Actors' Club.
- The Center for Jewish History, YIVO Institute for Jewish Research (see the Chelsea and Midtown chapter for information).

Village East Cinemas (Former Yiddish Theater)
181–189 Second Avenue (at Twelfth Street)
Web site: www.villageeastcinema.com
Subway: 4, 5, or 6 train to Union Square

At first glance, you may think this has always been an independent film house. Look closely and you will see clues of its Yiddish theater past. Stand on Twelfth Street and view the side of the building. It looks as though it was once a theater. The plaque on the front notes that the building was constructed in 1926. The main theater's ceiling carries a prominent Star of David.

In the heart of the Jewish Rialto district in 1926, Louis Jaffe, a Brooklyn lawyer and Jewish community leader, "designed the elaborate 1,265-seat live theater for Yiddish theater pioneer Maurice Schwartz."[3] Though built for entertainment, it borrowed several design and architectural elements popular in synagogues at the time. These included the Moorish Revival style, the ornamental ceiling, and the presence of the Star of David.

Yiddish star Maurice Schwartz drew crowds to productions such as *The Tenth Commandment* (1926) and *Yoshe Kalb* (1932), one of the longest-running shows at the theater. According to Village East Cinema records, "guests included Albert Einstein, Charlie Chaplin, George Gershwin, and New York City mayor Fiorello LaGuardia."[4]

As the neighborhood changed and interest in Yiddish theater dwindled, the building's function altered. No longer showing Yiddish productions, the theater housed mainstream musicals such as *The Best Little Whorehouse in Texas* and *Grease*. For a time, it was known as the Stuyvesant Theater and later the Phoenix Theater, an East Village landmark. In 1992, it reopened as Village East Cinemas, a sister company to the Angelika, showing indie films.

Former Café Royale
190 Second Avenue (at Twelfth Street)

Constructed in 1903, this otherwise unremarkable building housed the legendary Café Royal on the ground floor. From 1908 to 1952, the café brought together notable artists and writers, as well as Yiddish theater stars.

The Greenwich Village Society for Historic Preservation notes that "when lower Second Avenue was the heart of New York's Yiddish Rialto, Café Royal was the stomping ground of its stars." In 1939 the *New York Times* called the café "the Delmonico's, the Simpson's and the Fouquet's of Second Avenue, all in one."[5] "Everybody who is anybody in the creative Jewish world turns up at the Café Royal at least one night a week," the *New Yorker* remarked. "To be seen there is a social duty, a mark of distinction, and an investment in prestige."[6]

Folksbiene (National Yiddish Theatre)
Locations vary but include CUNY at Twenty-Fifth Street and
    Lexington
Telephone: (212) 213-2120
Web site: www.nationalyiddishtheatre.org

While the other Yiddish theaters in the old Jewish Rialto district are gone, the Folksbiene, remains. It has performed Yiddish plays continually since 1915. It is one of the most active Yiddish theaters in the world. The Folksbiene (literally, "People's Stage") does not at present have its own space, so it performs at a variety of theaters such as at CUNY. Its administrative offices are near Penn Station but not open to the public.

Check the Web site for performances, concerts, and lectures. This is a rare chance to see live Yiddish theater. Do not worry if you cannot understand the language. Subtitles in English and Russian are shown during each scene. Typically, there is a major show in the fall or spring, with several concerts and smaller shows performed throughout the year. Shows range from new or revived Yiddish musicals and plays centering on Purim themes to dramas relevant to modern issues. The Folksbiene's mission is to "preserve, promote and

Recent production of the Folksbeine's Golden Land. *Photograph by Michael Priest Photography.* (Courtesy National Yiddish Theatre—Folksbiene)

develop Yiddish theatre for current and future generations and to enhance the understanding of Yiddish culture as a vital component of Jewish Life."[7] From the beginning, it has been a nonprofit theater company that strives to produce socially relevant plays.

Background

The Folksbiene was created by nonprofessional workers such as tailors and hat makers with a passion for Yiddish literary works.

Artistic Director Zalmen Mlotek explains the cultural significance of the Yiddish theater: "More than the synagogue, the theater was the place for this immigrant population to come together. In the theater, they saw their lives depicted. They could laugh and cry there. They could see people they had not seen in a long time."

In the early twentieth century, when every genre of Yiddish theater was performed, patrons were fiercely devoted to particular actors. Mlotek notes, "Fights broke out in cafés among patrons about who were the best performers." He recounts a story of an actress who visited a patron who had been jailed for fighting for her.

The Folksbiene has survived for decades since the decline of Yiddish theater. In the 1950s and 1960s, it typically produced one show per season, which was about twenty weeks, usually performing on weekends. The Folksbiene performed every year, sometimes on a shoestring budget. Performances were held at the former Forward building (see "Lower East Side" chapter). In the mid-1970s, when the *Forward* left the neighborhood, performances were presented in an annex of the Upper East Side's Central Synagogue. But in the mid-1990s, the synagogue burned down, and congregants needed the annex space.

Today, the Folksbiene hopes to open a permanent space for Yiddish theater. For the last several seasons, City University and Baruch College hosted performances. Typically, there are two to three shows per season.

Bryna Wasserman, executive director of the National Yiddish Theatre, notes that the Folksbiene's goal is not just to put on shows but deliver the context surrounding them. "Each play has a universe around it. It's a matter of exploring the issues around the plays. The choices of the plays have distinct reasons." Recent themes have included the struggles of Soviet and African-American Jewry. Remarkably, many of the actors have little or no previous knowledge of Yiddish. But interest among them is high; 700 actors auditioned for a recent show. Rehearsal periods are only four weeks.

Call the box office or visit the Web site to purchase theater tickets. Memberships are also available.

Hebrew Actors' Union Building
31 East Seventh Street
Subway: 4, 5, or 6 train to Union Square

The Hebrew Actors' Union building, though in disrepair, is one of the few remnants of the Yiddish theater era. In 2005, with no leader and declining membership, the Hebrew Actors' Union was proclaimed "defunct" by the presiding body Associated Actors and Artists of America.

Mike Burstyn, a surviving Yiddish actor, often prowled the union's second floor as a child. He described the scene then as "a clubroom perpetually filled with smoke, egos, and games of pinochle and rummy." When he revisited many decades later, he found "shelves and cupboards full of plays, photographs, union records, costumes, and yellowing scores by leading Yiddish composers such as Sholom Secunda and Alexander Olshanetsky, all desperately in need of rescue."[8] Since then, Burstyn has spearheaded an effort to preserve the material.

Some want to sell the building, while others want to convert it into a Yiddish theater center for research and possibly a museum.

Background

Jewish labor leader Joseph Barondess founded the Hebrew Actors' Union (HAU) in 1899 for actors in Yiddish theater. A 1925 article in the *New York Times* titled "The Yiddish Stage" portrayed the organization as having "at that time over three hundred members, and notes that it has not only placed all of its members in good positions, but [that] it has also granted many privileges to non-members." It also stated that "a great many members of the union are American-born and all of them are thoroughly Americanized."[9]

Yiddish Theater Stars' Walk of Fame
156 Second Avenue (at Tenth Street)
Subway: 4, 5, or 6 train to Union Square

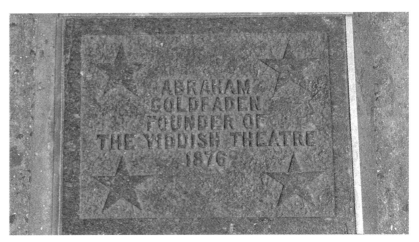

Abraham Goldfaden is represented in the Yiddish Theater Stars' Walk of Fame on Second Avenue at Tenth Street.

Another clue to the neighborhood's Yiddish theater past rests in front of the former location of the Second Avenue Deli. Look at the sidewalk and see the area's version of the Hollywood Walk of Fame—the Yiddish Theater Stars' Walk of Fame. Check out the stars bearing the names of David Kessler, Lucy Gehrman, Henrietta Jacobson, Molly Picon, and more. The inscriptions are faded, but you can still make them out. When the Second Avenue Deli stood at this location, a sign above its doors read, "This star-studded sidewalk was created to immortalize the great actors, actresses and musicians who graced the stages of the eight Yiddish theaters that once flourished along Second Avenue."[10]

Former Commodore Theater
Second Avenue (at Sixth Street)

This may be the only building in the world that has housed a Yiddish theater, cinema, playhouse, famed rock 'n' roll venue, exclusive gay club, and local bank. Erected in 1926 as a performance venue for Yiddish dramatic productions in the flourishing Jewish Rialto district, the Commodore Theater has since taken on numerous incarnations. In many ways, its various functions have mirrored the dramatic changes in the neighborhood. Built during the 1920s building craze, it capitalized on the vibrant Yiddish theater movement. When the Jewish population dwindled, the building was put to use as a movie theater, due to the growing popularity of the new art form. Later, it made use of its theatrical structure to show mainstream plays. The late 1960s and early 1970s brought rock 'n' roll, and the Fillmore East—the "Church of Rock and Roll"—was born at the former Yiddish theater. The same stage that once stood beneath the feet of Yiddish-theater actors now hosted musical icons John Lennon; Frank Zappa and the Mothers of Invention; the Allman Brothers Band; Jefferson Airplane; Crosby, Stills, Nash and Young; and Led Zeppelin.

Audiences' tastes changed once again, and some of the music became less popular. Theater promoters decided to close the venue. During the decline of the city in the late 1970s, the building was scarcely used. The rise of gay culture at this time breathed new life into it. In 1980, the Saint, an exclusive gay disco, opened in this former theater and music space. The club was more lively and famous than many others, but the management overspent and enjoyed only limited revenues, due to its exclusivity. Patronage also declined because of the AIDS epidemic, whose casualties included the club's owner. It closed in the late 1980s with a bang comparable to the Fillmore East's exit, in this case a forty-eight-hour, nonstop disco party. In the 1990s, the building had several short-lived uses and eventually stood vacant until the auditorium was demolished in 1996. As the neighborhood gentrified and financial services became the primary industry of the city, the building, too, remade itself. In 2007, a branch of Emigrant Bank moved in. One has to wonder whether customers standing in the bank's lobby have any idea what had come before in this space.

Tip for the Visitor: In the lobby of Emigrant Bank, you can view images on the wall showing the building's days as a Yiddish theater, cinema, playhouse, rock club, and gay disco.

Former Orpheum at St. Mark's Place
Second Avenue (between Seventh Street and St. Mark's Place)

Today, this is an off-Broadway theater showing fast-moving dance productions such as *Stomp*. Like so many other buildings in the neighborhood, it served several purposes over the years. Its original use is unknown, though it is speculated that it was a concert garden in the 1880s. Later, it was a women's medical college. Converted to a Yiddish theater in the early twentieth century, it was showing films by the 1920s. Like many theaters in the neighborhood, it converted back to dramatic productions in 1958.

Former Public Theater
Second Avenue (between Third and Fourth streets)

Opened in 1926, this was one of the later Yiddish theaters on the Jewish Rialto. According to some accounts, two candy vendors from the former People's Theatre on the Bowery created this theater. The venue showed other genres of Yiddish performance, including vaudeville and films.

Like many neighborhood theaters, this former Yiddish theater presented mainstream plays as well. When the local Puerto Rican population increased in the 1950s, it began to show many Spanish-language films. In late 1957 it reopened as the Anderson Theatre and continued to run Yiddish programs until the 1960s.

Reflecting the increased interest in punk music in the 1970s, the venue hosted punk rock concerts, but by 1979 it was no longer being used. In 1990, the theater was partially demolished, and in 1997 the remaining portions were turned into apartments. You can still view the onetime Yiddish theater building's exterior.

Former Second Avenue Theater
35–37 Second Avenue (between First and Second streets)

Opened in 1911, the Second Avenue Theater was among the first of the Yiddish theaters in the Jewish Rialto. It served as a place where emerging Yiddish actors tweaked their craft and, in some cases, gained mentorship. David Kessler was a key personage of the theater and is said to have aided the careers of Yiddish-theater icons Maurice Schwartz, Bertha Gerstein, and Celia Adler. Kessler attempted to increase the quality of the plays presented, some of which were seen as lowbrow and burdened by stock characters. Like other theaters, this building also screened movies.

In the 1950s after Yiddish theater had lost much of its glitter, Yiddish star Molly Picon joined with other notable Yiddish-theater actors in commemorating the seventy-fifth anniversary of the genre.[11] A few years later, the theater was demolished to make room for a parking lot.

Places of Interest

Hebrew Immigrant Aid Society Building
425 Lafayette Street
Telephone: (212) 967-4100
Web site: www.hias.org
Subway: 6 train to Lafayette Street

Strolling by the famed Joseph Papp Public Theater, you may not realize its historic importance to immigrants in bygone days. This building was constructed in 1853 as the Astor Library, which later became part of the New York Public Library. In the 1880s, the building was turned into the headquarters of the Hebrew Immigrant Aid Society (HIAS), where lawyers and social workers helped Jewish newcomers navigate the bureaucracy of immigration. Specifically, they provided financial assistance, helped interpret for those with limited English, and aided immigrants in finding housing and work.

In the late 1960s the building was converted into a theater for Joseph Papp's New York Shakespeare Festival and the Public Theater. Plays staged here tended to be more alternative given its nonprofit status, but the theater also launched future Broadway blockbusters, including *A Chorus Line* and *Hair*.

Background

With the local explosion of the Eastern European Jewish population in the early 1880s, the social, financial, and language needs of the immigrants grew exponentially. In 1881, the society was founded to resettle and assist these new arrivals. Since its inception, HIAS claims to have rescued and/or resettled nearly 4.5 million people.[12]

Emma Lazarus, author of "The New Colossus," the poem written on the Statue of Liberty, was a famous volunteer here in the early days. (See "Lower Manhattan" chapter, Emma Lazarus Memorial Plaque.)

In the wake of World War II, HIAS assisted about 300,000 displaced Jews, and during the 1950s and 1960s it aided Jewish refugees of the Soviet invasion of Hungary and of the Egyptian and Cuban revolutions. In the 1970s and 1980s, a major focus was on the plight of refugees from the Soviet Union, and in more recent years the society has assisted immigrants from Latin America, the Caribbean, Africa, and Asia.

Hebrew Union College
One West Fourth Street (between Broadway and Mercer)
Open Monday-Thursday 9 a.m.–5 p.m.
Admission: Free but government-issued ID required
Web site: www.huc.org
Subway: 6 train to Astor Place

Nestled among New York University's buildings is the primary seminary for rabbis, cantors, and educators in the Reform movement. The other branches in the United States are located in Cincinnati and Los Angeles.

As you enter the seminary, visit the HUC-JIR Museum, which includes a rare-book room, an archives gallery, and a variety of art, photography, and historical exhibits. Past exhibits included "A Stitch in Jewish Time: Provocative Textiles," "Torahluminations: The Art of Peter Asher Pitzele," "Envisioning Maps," and "Countdown to Perfection—Meditations."

Inquire about lecture programs open to the public. If you like music, ask about the occasional concerts in the auditorium performed by local Yiddish choirs.

Site of Peter Stuyvesant Home
Second Avenue and East Tenth Street

Somewhat ironically placed in what would later be a thriving Jewish neighborhood, Peter Stuyvesant's mansion once stood on the site of St. Mark's-in-the-Bowery Church. He was the governor of Dutch New Amsterdam when the first twenty-three Jewish refugees arrived in 1654 from northern Brazil. Fearing they would be a great burden, he requested permission from Holland to expel them, but his request was denied.

Russian Turkish Baths

268 East Tenth Street (between First Avenue and Avenue A)
Open (generally) noon–10 p.m.
Telephone: (212) 674-9250
Web site: www.russianturkishbaths.com

After walking around to these sites, you may need some relaxation.
The Russian Turkish Baths have been offering steam rooms and
baths since 1892. Stop by for a Swedish/Russian massage, Thai
massage, or black mud treatment. Or visit the Russian sauna,
Turkish room, or ice-cold pool. Some days are only open to one
gender, so be sure to call before going.

Triangle Shirtwaist Factory Fire Site

Corner of Washington Place and Greene Street
Subway: 6 train to Astor Place

Walking through the New York University buildings near

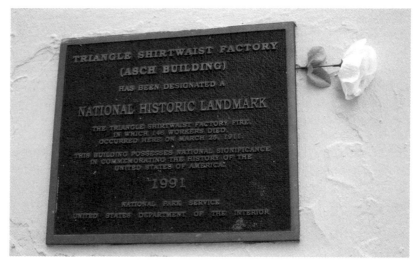

*Plaque commemorating the Triangle Shirtwaist Factory fire of March
25, 1911, in which 146 garment-industry employees lost their lives, with
many others injured. The fire is considered a catalyst for workplace safety
regulations.* (Photograph by Jessica Siemens.)

Washington Square Park, you may not realize that, about a century ago, an event so gruesome took place here that it fundamentally changed human and worker rights in the U.S. It is a story of greed, workplace conditions, and the justice system. When standing in front of the Asch Building, look up to the eighth, ninth, and tenth floors and remember that this is the site of one of New York's three great disasters, along with the sinking of the *General Slocum* in 1904 and the obliteration of the World Trade Center on September 11, 2001. On these floors, the Triangle Shirtwaist Factory, a manufacturer of women's blouses, employed about five hundred workers, most of them young immigrants. The neighborhood had become a center for garment manufacturers because it offered more space than the Lower East Side's apartment factories. The employees toiled away for long hours for very little pay, in the inhumane conditions typical of this period.

Workers had been struggling for rights against this backdrop. Many protested and some sought to form unions, but the garment bosses often sent men to beat up and intimidate protesters. Many employers threatened employees with immediate dismissal if they were ever caught even discussing joining a union. In the first decade of the twentieth century, the International Ladies' Garment Workers' Union played a key role in demanding safer conditions, but their cries for change were largely ignored. It was not until one of the city's worst tragedies occurred that any true reform would take place.

The Fire

The infamous Triangle Shirtwaist Factory fire occurred just before closing, at 4:45 p.m. on March 25, 1911. In those days, factory owners usually locked the exits to ensure that employees did not steal. This dangerous practice exacerbated the tragedy as workers tried, and were unable, to escape the fire—146 textile employees perished either from the fire or from leaping out of the window. Whether the owners knew that the doors were locked and their workers would be trapped was a question explored during the trial.

Most of the employees were recent Jewish and Italian immigrant female workers in their late teens or early to mid-twenties. Barry

Feldman, New York historian and tour guide, explains that the garment workers were typically Italian mothers and children, many as young as fifteen. Some made the long commute from the Upper East Side.

The city's fire marshal concluded that "the likely cause of the fire was an unextinguished match or cigarette butt in the scrap bin, which by the time of the fire held two months' worth of accumulated cuttings," although a *New York Times* article suggested that "it may have been started by the engines that ran the sewing machines overheating."[13] The fire department's ladders could not reach even the sixth floor.

Ironically, the owners of the factory, Max Blanck and Isaac Harris, had once been sweatshop workers themselves. Feldman explains their rise from "sweaters" to owners:

> They worked in tenements as contractors as they worked from home and supervised others. They then rented factory space. The building itself was a vast improvement over the small tenements in which people had worked prior. The irony is that they came from the same circumstances. They thought they were living the American dream.

The Trial

The owners escaped the fire through the roof. Later, they were indicted on charges of manslaughter. They hired famous defense attorneys who argued to the jury that "witnesses memorized their statements and were told what to say by the prosecutors." A key point of deliberation was whether the owners knew that the doors were locked at the time. The government could not prove this point beyond a reasonable doubt.

Excerpt from the testimony of Ethel Monick, age sixteen, a ninth-floor worker: "I seen the fire and then I seen all the girls rushing down to the place to escape. So I tried to go through the Greene Street door, and there were quick girls there and I seen I can't get out there, so I went to the elevator, and then I heard the elevator fall down, so I ran

> through to the Washington Place side, and I went over
> to the Washington Place side and there wasn't any girls
> there. . . . So I went over to the door. I tried the door and
> I could not open it, so I thought I was not strong enough
> to open it, so I hollered girls here is a door, and they all
> rushed over and they tried to open it, but it was locked
> and they hollered the door is locked and we can't open it!"

The jury acquitted the two factory owners, and victims' survivors
were paid a paltry $75 per deceased worker. Ironically, the owners
actually benefitted from the tragedy. Historical documents show
that their insurance company paid "about $60,000 more than their
reported losses." In 1913, Blanck was re-arrested for "locking the
door in his factory during working hours" and was fined $20.[14]

The Legacy

One positive outcome is that this tragedy spawned legislation
mandating better working conditions and helped empower the
International Ladies' Garment Workers' Union, resulting in
improved labor conditions. Today, the Remember the Triangle
Fire Coalition is an alliance of more than two hundred organizations
and individuals dedicated to memorializing and raising public
awareness about the tragedy.

Historic Synagogues

Sixth Street Community Synagogue (Orthodox)
325 East Sixth Street (between First and Second avenues)
Telephone: (212) 473-3665
Web site: www.sixthstreetsynagogue.org
Subway: 6 train to Astor Place

Like many synagogues in the area, this one began in 1848 as
a United German Lutheran church. In 1940, it became the
Community Synagogue.

The church is associated with one of New York's largest maritime disasters, second only to the *Titanic*. The disaster is the third largest in New York City history, after the terrorist attacks of September 11, 2001, and the Triangle Shirtwaist Factory fire of March 25, 1911. The records of the Sixth Street Community Synagogue summarize the tragedy: "On June 15, 1904, about 1,200 mostly German congregants from St. Mark's Evangelical Lutheran Church died when the excursion steamship *General Slocum*, which was taking the congregants on a day trip, caught fire and sank in the East River. At the time, it was New York City's deadliest disaster. It traumatized the community and hastened residents' flight to uptown areas like Yorkville." Today, the tragedy is not well known, and, partly to increase awareness, a 100th anniversary memorial ceremony was conducted in 2004.

Tip for the Visitor: Check the Web site for information about the weekly klezmer concerts. Klezmer jam sessions, Yiddish classes, and Yiddish dance parties also take place at the synagogue on a regular basis.

Eateries

Moishe's Bakery (Kosher)
115 Second Avenue (between Sixth and Seventh Street)
Telephone: (212) 505-8555
Prices: Inexpensive
Subway: 4, 5, or 6 train to Union Square

Moishe's is one of the last kosher bakeries in the area. Enjoy the rugelach, mandelbrot, babka, and other treats. Customers recommend the prune Danish.

Little Poland Restaurant
200 Second Avenue (at Twelfth Street)
Telephone: (212) 777-9728
Prices: Moderate
Subway: 4, 5, or 6 train to Union Square

This restaurant specializes in Polish food, some of which has crossed over to Ashkenazi Jewish food. Specialties include red borscht, fresh cabbage soup, potato lamb soup, kasha, potato pancakes, bigos (a mixture of meats), kielbasa with sauerkraut, and potato dumplings with mushroom sauce.

Veselka's
144 Second Avenue (at Ninth Street) (also 9 East First Street at
    Bowery)
Telephone: (212) 228-9682
Web site: www.veselka.com
Price: Moderate
Subway: 4, 5, or 6 train to Union Square

Veselka's specializes in Ukrainian food such as pierogies, filled with spinach, goat cheese, pumpkin, mushrooms, or other choices. Other specialties include beef stroganoff, stuffed cabbage, and Ukrainian meatballs.

Established in 1954 by Ukrainian-born Wolodymyr Darmochwal, Veselka's started as a humble neighborhood candy store. It had a newsstand and a small counter where customers ate Ukrainian dishes. The restaurant expanded and today serves a plethora of homemade Ukrainian dishes.

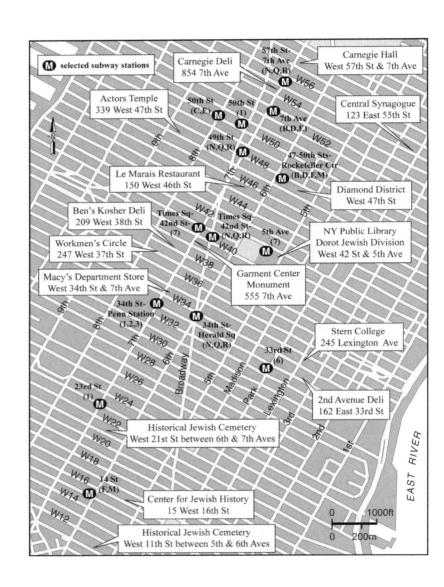

M selected subway stations

Carnegie Deli
854 7th Ave

57th St-
7th Ave
(N,Q,R)
M W56

Carnegie Hall
West 57th St & 7th Ave

Actors Temple
339 West 47th St

W54

50th St
(C,E)
M

50th St
(1)
M

M
7th Ave
(B,D,E)

Central Synagogue
123 East 55th St

W52

49th St
(N,Q,R)
M W50

W48

47-50th Sts-
Rockefeller Ctr
M (B,D,F,M)

Le Marais Restaurant
150 West 46th St

7th

W46

6th

Diamond District
West 47th St

W44

Ben's Kosher Deli
209 West 38th St

Times Sq-
42nd St-
(7)
M

W42

Times Sq-
42nd St-
M (N,Q,R)

5th

5th Ave
(7)

NY Public Library
Dorot Jewish Division
West 42 St & 5th Ave

Workmen's Circle
247 West 37th St

M
W40

W38

M

Macy's Department Store
West 34th St & 7th Ave

W36

Garment Center
Monument
555 7th Ave

34th St-
Penn Station
(1,2,3)
M

W34

8th

7th

W32

M

34th St-
Herald Sq
(N,Q,R)

Stern College
245 Lexington Ave

9th

W30

6th

W28

Broadway

33rd St
(6)
M

W26

5th

Madison

Park

Lexington

23rd St
(1)
M

W24

2nd Avenue Deli
162 East 33rd St

W22

3rd

W20

Historical Jewish Cemetery
West 21st St between 6th & 7th Aves

2nd

1st

EAST RIVER

W18

W16

14 St
(F,M)
M

W14

Center for Jewish History
15 West 16th St

0   1000ft

W12

0   200m

Historical Jewish Cemetery
West 11th St between 5th & 6th Aves

Chelsea and Midtown

Stroll through the Garment District and view some of the lesser-known Jewish sites in these neighborhoods. Visit the vast archives at the Center for Jewish History, where you can peruse records or photos of Yiddish, Sephardic, German, and other Jewish peoples and cultures, or research your own family history. Take a tour of the impressive New York Public Library with its wealth of Jewish cultural archives and photos. Walk through the Diamond District and watch the "wheeling and dealing."

Museums

Center for Jewish History
15 West Sixteenth Street (between Fifth and Sixth avenues)
Open Sunday 11 a.m.–5 p.m., Monday and Wednesday 9:30 a.m.–
    8 p.m., Tuesday and Thursday 9:30 a.m.–5 p.m., Friday 9:30
    a.m.–3 p.m.
Admission: Some galleries charge; inquire at desk
Telephone: (212) 294-8301
Web site: www.cjh.org
Subway: 1, 2, or 3 train to Fourteenth Street

Think of the Center for Jewish History as a one-stop shop for collections from Jewish communities around the world. Nestled in a quiet Chelsea neighborhood, the Center is one of the globe's largest Jewish research institutions. It is an umbrella for five partner organizations—the American Jewish Historical Society, American Sephardi Federation, Leo Baeck Institute, Yeshiva University Museum, and YIVO Institute for Jewish Research. It notes that these collections "total more than 500,000 volumes and

100 million documents and include thousands of pieces of artwork, textiles, ritual objects, recordings, films, and photographs."[1]

As you enter, observe the mosaic floors with the designs of date trees, fig trees, wheat, and grapes. To the right is a composite of individual pieces of glass forming a luminous manuscript. The design displays an assortment of alphabets.

Start your visit by viewing the orientation film. It will provide an overview of the five partners, the Center's scholarship, and its ancestral research. The film traces the curation process of salvaging and preserving key texts.

Ask about upcoming speakers or events in the Center's auditorium. The first floor also houses a rare-books library. The remainder of the first and second floors is divided among exhibits from the five partners:[2]

The American Jewish Historical Society (AJHS) displays a history of the Jewish presence in the United States. It also has the handwritten original of Emma Lazarus's "The New Colossus," the poem inscribed on the Statue of Liberty.

The American Sephardi Federation (ASF) displays archives of American Sephardic and Mizrahi communities (Jews of Arabdescent).

The Leo Baeck Insititute documents the history and culture of German-speaking Jewry. It has temporary exhibits on key figures such as famous mathematicians.

The Yeshiva University Museum (YU Museum) showcases art and culture across different historical periods.

The YIVO Institute for Jewish Research (YIVO) exhibit explores the history and culture of Ashkenazi Jews and their influence in the U.S. It also traces Yiddish culture and scholarship from Central and Eastern Europe.[3]

Explore some of the centuries-old texts on display. View a Hebrew prayer book from 1716 Berlin, currency from the Middle Ages, and an illustrated, handmade manuscript from Prague in 1489. Also on display is a 1555 edict granting a man "the right to carry arms to defend himself."

Sports exhibits highlight the lives of important baseball figures such as Hank Greenberg and Major League Baseball commissioner Bud Selig. Look for Topps Company baseball trading cards from the mid-1950s.

If possible, go downstairs and watch how curators preserve archival materials. Look for the bubble-like incubators that take creases out of worn papers.

You can learn about your ancestors at the Center Genealogy Institute upstairs. Beforehand, find out the full names, locations, and key dates of ancestors you would like to inquire about. Call in advance to schedule appointments with the reference archivists to help you.

Nearby is the Lillian Goldman Reading Room, with a reference collection from the five partners. Enjoy the books in the room; they will not let you take them out.

Tips for the Visitor: If you are traveling with teenagers, be sure to visit the Teen Family History Program. Make an appointment with the librarians to help your teenager use the museum's technology to discover what it was like for their ancestors to come to America.

If you are visiting on a Tuesday or Thursday around 1 p.m., inquire about tours.

Places of Interest

Carnegie Hall
881 Seventh Avenue (corner of Fifty-Seventh Street)
Tours Monday-Friday 11:30 a.m., 12:30 p.m., 2 p.m., and 3 p.m.,
    Saturday 11:30 a.m. and 12:30 p.m., Sunday 12:30 p.m.
Admission: $10 per person; $8 students/seniors; $4 children under 12
Telephone: (212) 903-9765
Web site: www.carnegiehall.org
Subway: A, C, B, D, or 1 train to Fifty-Ninth Street/Columbus
    Circle; or N, Q, or R train to Fifty-Seventh Street/Seventh
    Avenue; or B, D, or E train to Seventh Avenue; or F train to
    Fifty-Seventh Street/Sixth Avenue

You have likely heard of or even visited Carnegie Hall, but you might be unaware of its Jewish connection. In the 1960s, the 1891 world-class concert hall was threatened with demolition after the Lincoln Center for the Performing Arts was completed nearby. Thanks to a campaign spearheaded by Jewish violinist Isaac Stern, the building was saved from the wrecking ball.

Carnegie Hall's unlikely beginning involves a conductor in his twenties. As Carnegie Hall history relates, "In the middle of the Atlantic, he convinced one of the world's richest men to build a music hall in an undeveloped section of upper Manhattan." In 1887, the industrial magnate Andrew Carnegie and his new wife, Louise Whitfield, were sailing from New York to London. By coincidence, the accomplished twenty-five-year-old conductor at the Metropolitan Opera, Walter Damrosch, was also on the ship.[4] An unlikely friendship evolved. After this fortuitous meeting, the three stayed in close contact, and on subsequent visits to Carnegie in Scotland, Damrosch outlined his ideas. Carnegie's curiosity was piqued. He decided the venture was worthy and agreed to significantly fund construction of Damrosch's project. Carnegie Hall was born.[5]

In 1890, Damrosch's vision of a world-class music venue became a reality. Carnegie is said to have declared, "It is built to stand for ages, and during these ages it is probable that this hall will intertwine itself with the history of our country."[6] He was half-right. The institution certainly did bring together the nation's most important political figures, authors, and intellectuals, including Woodrow Wilson, Theodore Roosevelt, and Mark Twain, but despite his best wishes, the iconic concert hall came close to demolition.

After decades of celebrated use, by the mid-1950s the venue was in trouble. At that time city planners often put function ahead of aesthetics, and historical preservation committees did not have the political clout they enjoy today. Against this backdrop, the music world was changing, and Carnegie Hall was slow to adapt. Though the hall's owner, Robert Simon, wanted to keep the venue going, financial realities forced him to list the property for sale in 1956. No deals to save it were forthcoming, and by 1960, the building was slated for demolition.

But here the story takes a twist. At the last minute, Isaac Stern and his grassroots organization Citizens Committee for Carnegie

Hall were able to halt the impending destruction of the historic venue. Potential ownership shifted from the private to the public sphere. The city bought the famed music hall for $5 million.[7] Andrew Carnegie's vision would survive. And the public would keep an extraordinary musical venue.

Tip for the Visitor: Many Carnegie Hall audience members do not realize that they can get a behind-the-scenes tour. To see how the world-class music institution comes together for riveting performances, inquire at the box office.

Cemetery of Shearith Israel
Twenty-First Street between Sixth and Seventh avenues

Cemeteries are a rare sight in Manhattan, yet several remain from the days before the city banned them on the island. The oldest synagogue in the United States, Shearith Israel, placed four cemeteries in Manhattan. The location of the first is unknown, the second is in Chatham Square (see Lower Manhattan chapter), the third is on Eleventh Street just east of Sixth Avenue, and the fourth is in modern-day Chelsea at Twenty-First Street between Sixth and Seventh avenues.

The cemeteries are gated, but you can look in. The tranquil grounds stand in contrast to the surrounding bustling streets.

Garment Center Neighborhood
Between Sixth and Ninth avenues and Thirty-Fourth and Forty-Second streets

Clothing manufacturers once dotted this landscape. Sweatshop workers toiled in factories. Runners carted materials and clothing between manufacturers. Wholesalers peddled accessories such as buttons. The neighborhood whirred with activity.

Most clothing manufacturers have moved their operations to developing countries. Yet the neighborhood retains vestiges of its sartorial past. Prominent fashion designers station their headquarters in or near this neighborhood. Walking through it you can view the remaining clothes-supply and materials shops, some of which have been featured on reality TV shows such as *Project Runway*, as well as the Fashion Institute of Technology. If you explore the neighborhood during the day, you may run into clothing racks speeding down the crowded sidewalks, historic warehouse spaces, or designers and buyers inspecting showrooms.[8]

If you're interested in reading more about the Garment District, try the book *A Stitch in Time*, from the Fashion Center Business Improvement District (BID).

Garment Center Monument
555 Seventh Avenue (between Thirty-Ninth and Fortieth streets)
Subway: 1, 2, or 3 train to Forty-Second Street

This striking sculpture, designed by Judith Weller in 1984, depicts a garment worker bent over his machine, painstakingly sewing clothing.

Diamond District Area
West Forty-Seventh Street between Fifth and Sixth avenues
Open mostly Sunday-Friday afternoon

Walk along West Forty-Seventh Street between Fifth and Sixth avenues and observe the unique culture of diamond selling in the Diamond District. Diamond dealers, sellers, and buyers trade, while sidewalk retailers hawk their wares. Tucked away is the famed Geological Institute of America, which provides instruction to budding dealers of precious stones.

Note the unique blend of business and religion. For example, many deals are concluded by a "blessing and a handshake" (*mazel und brucha*). Commerce and religion also meet in the elite and somewhat secretive Diamond Dealers Club (DDC), which has its own synagogue.[9]

In the early 1940s, as many businesses and people moved uptown, so did the Diamond District. Previously, it had existed in two locales: near Canal and Bowery and in the Financial District near Fulton Street. While this geographic shift was occurring, so was a demographic one. The invasion of the Netherlands and Belgium during the Second World War led to many in the

Garment Center Monument. (Photograph by Jessica Siemens.)

European diamond industry fleeing to New York. After the war, a number of them stayed. Indeed, Orthodox Jewry has a profound presence in the Diamond District today.

> Tip for the Visitor: About nine out of ten diamonds entering the United States come through New York. According to some reports, total revenue for a single day's trading averages $400 million across the 2,600 enterprises in the Diamond District.[10]

Macy's Department Store
Thirty-Fourth Street and Broadway
Subway: 1, 2, or 3 train to Thirty-Fourth Street

Endless sales. The Thanksgiving Day Parade. Midrange department store. These are likely your associations with Macy's. All are true. But did you know that the flagship Macy's Department Store was built on the site of Congregation B'nai Jeshurun, New York's second-oldest congregation (after the Spanish and Portuguese Synagogue) and first Ashkenazic congregation, organized in 1825?

Background
Macy's started as R. H. Macy Dry Goods on Sixth Avenue and Fourteenth Street in what was then the fashionable Ladies' Mile district. In 1888, Isidor Straus and his brother Nathan sold their crockery and glassware shop and acquired equity in Macy's. They became co-owners in 1896.

At the turn of the twentieth century, the expanding department store relocated to its current location. Since this move inconvenienced customers who planned to shop in both the department store and the company's other dry-goods emporium about twenty blocks south, the management provided a steam wagonette to transport shoppers between the stores.[11]

Sadly, Isidor and his wife, Judith Straus, perished in the historic sinking of the *Titanic* on her maiden voyage, on April 15, 1912.

This lamppost with a diamond shape on top marks the renowned Diamond District. (Photograph by Jessica Siemens.)

New York Public Library—Dorot Jewish Division
Fifth Avenue and Forty-Second Street
Open Monday and Thursday-Saturday 10 a.m.–5:45 p.m.,
   Tuesday-Wednesday 10 a.m.–7:15 p.m., or by appointment
   with the research specialist
Telephone: (212) 930-0601
Web site: www.nypl.org/locations/schwarzman/jewish-division
Subway: 4, 5, or 6, or S train to Grand Central

Just a block from Grand Central Station stands one of the most
beautiful and voluminous public libraries in the world. On either
side of the grand staircase outside the main entrance, a sculpture
of a lion welcomes visitors. Roam the marble-walled hallways
and consider a tour of the sprawling structure to view the DeWitt
Wallace Room, the Map Room, and many others.

What connects the library to Jewish history is the Dorot Jewish
Division, which houses one of the world's most comprehensive
collections of Hebraica and Judaica.[12] As you enter the Dorot Room
through the DeWitt Wallace Room, notice the figures on the wall
symbolizing scholarship and education. The wooded brown ceiling
and panels adorned with decorative arts add to the décor.

The NYPL public-relations official notes that the collection
comprises "400,000 books, periodicals, journals, microforms,
electronic (online) resources, rare books, manuscripts, photographs,
sheet music, theater programs, and examples of everything else
that can appear in a library collection, in all languages of Jewish
creativity and scholarship."

Glance through the latest acquisitions. Works with titles such
as "Modern Ladino Culture: Press, Belles Lettres and Theater
in the Late Ottomon Empire" may be esoteric but can be a
goldmine for research or scholarship. The library does not allow
you to check out these books, so you will need to read materials
there. Also, you will need to look up the call number and give it
to the reference library to retrieve anything from their collection.
Turnaround time is about twenty-four hours, so see if you can find
it beforehand on the Web site.[13]

The collection is best known for books on Jewish immigration
to New York, Yiddish theater, and the Holocaust, illuminated

manuscripts, oral histories, and Jewish newspapers from around the world. For visually-oriented visitors, look up the collection's noted photographs from the Middle East.[14]

Background

The Dorot Jewish Division of the New York Public Library was established in November 1897 when philanthropist Jacob Schiff donated $10,000 for the purchase of Semitic literature. The library acquired several private libraries, including those of Leon Mandelstamm, Meyer Lehren, and Isaac Meyer, and holdings from Astor. By the early 1900s, the Dorot Jewish Division was considered one of the best Jewish libraries in the world.[15]

Stern College for Women at Yeshiva University
245 Lexington Avenue at Thirty-Third Street
Telephone: (646) 592-4150
Web site: www.yu.edu/stern

Established in 1954 as the women's counterpart to Yeshiva University, Stern College for Women (SCW) offers Jewish scholarship combined with liberal-arts subjects. Though well known today, it had humble beginnings. Its first class comprised thirty-two students at 253 Lexington Avenue, formerly the Packard Junior College. Students lived at various nearby hotels until the mid-1960s, when the school acquired dorms.[16] (See the Washington Heights chapter for more information on Yeshiva University.)

Workmen's Circle (Arbeiter Ring)
247 West Thirty-Seventh Street, Fifth Floor
Telephone: (212) 889-6800
Web site: www.circle.org

Created about a century ago, the Workmen's Circle was once a household name among Jewish immigrants. It played an important role in advocating for Jewish cultural, social, and economic-justice causes. It helped settle new arrivals who mostly spoke Yiddish.

Today, the organization strives to reinvigorate Yiddish language and culture. It is struggling with a dwindling membership and the challenge of staying relevant. As such, it concentrates on contemporary issues, including immigrant rights, labor conditions, and healthcare policies. It also offers educational workshops and programs on Yiddish culture.

Check the Web site for events such as concerts, literary discussions, or political talks.[17] The offices are otherwise closed to the public.

Historic Synagogues

Actor's Temple (Post-Denominational)
339 West Forty-Seventh Street
Telephone: (212) 245-6975
Web site: www.theactorstemple.org
Subway: 1, 2, or 3 train to Forty-Second Street

Classic Hollywood names of yesteryear—Red Buttons, Milton Berle, the Three Stooges—once belonged to this century-old synagogue. It still stands in the ever-changing Hell's Kitchen neighborhood. You can see vestiges of its Hollywood past in the pictures that line the interior stairwell. Look for the memorial to Jewish Broadway actress Sophie Tucker.[18]

Background

Founded in 1917, the Actor's Temple was first known as the "West Side Hebrew Relief Association."[19] At the time, this busy neighborhood, home to a steamship port, was gritty and somewhat dangerous. As more actors moved into the area, the synagogue became an "Actor's Temple." Shelley Winters, Jack Benny, Milton Berle, Red Buttons, Eddie Cantor, and members of the original Three Stooges attended services. Jill Hausman, rabbi of the Actor's Temple, describes how the rabbi at the time courted members from the entertainment industry:

> Rabbi Birstein was interested in recruiting Sophie Tucker as a congregant. He attended her shows and asked her to visit. She was very reluctant. But his persistence paid off and she finally agreed.

At the time, actors were not necessarily welcome in "High Society" temples, so this was a place where anyone in that field could worship.

Sophie Tucker became an active congregant. Shortly thereafter, Red Buttons joined. Actors such as Milton Berle, Edward G. Robinson, and Eddie Cantor soon followed, along with producers, agents, and other members of the industry. Benefits were held that featured household names, including Frank Sinatra and Louis Armstrong. Jill Hausman notes that the Temple became a "slice of old New York, not just a Jewish place."

But, beginning during the Great Depression and accelerating during World War II, the neighborhood's glamorous population of vaudeville and musical-theater actors faded as nightclubs closed, television production moved to California, and vaudeville disappeared. The Times Square area deteriorated and the Actor's Temple along with it. As a *New York Times* article about the synagogue put it, "Actors, talent agents, and Broadway-area businessmen who had once helped fill the synagogue's pews and pay its bills, and organized annual benefits, departed for the suburbs or the greener work pastures of Hollywood."[20]

Today, this trend has reversed. In recent years, the neighborhood has made a dramatic turnaround. Times Square has been rejuvenated, though critics will point out its lack of cultural uniqueness. But while the Actor's Temple has shown a modest uptick in membership, it is struggling to keep up financially.

To increase revenue, the Temple serves a double purpose today: as a synagogue and as an off-Broadway performance space for such shows as *After Anne Frank* and *Zero Hour*. Today's congregation includes actors and comedians. Some recent events have included a Jewish-themed slide show and storytelling and comedy benefits.

The Actor's Temple contains physical reminders of the synagogue's past. Photographs line the stairwell, many of them original headshots from the Temple's archive of famous former members such as the Three Stooges. Plaques bear the names of Jack Benny and other congregants. A stained-glass window features Sophie Tucker's name, while those of Joe E. Lewis and the Friar's Club grace another. There are also eleven Torahs with five crowns, harkening back to the Temple's glory days.

Tip for the Visitor: A November 2011 *New York Times* article on the Actor's Temple noted this interesting story: "Sophie Tucker, the self-proclaimed *Last of the Red Hot Mamas* who was famous for her vaudeville renditions of *Some of These Days*, and *My Yiddishe Momme*, was sitting in the women's balcony during the High Holy Days and spotted a wealthy woman she was acquainted with enter the men's section below to pray with her husband, causing something of a stir. The formidable Tucker rose, marched downstairs and joined her, making an emphatic statement that the rabbi was loath to challenge. From then on, more women and men sat together."[21]

Central Synagogue (Reform)

652 Lexington Avenue (at Fifty-Fifth Street)
Telephone: (212) 838-5123
Web site: www.centralsynagogue.org
Subway: 6 train to Fifty-First Street; or 4, 5, or E train to Fifty-Ninth Street

In the middle of the commercial hustle and bustle of Midtown East stands an impressively ornate structure. Its Moorish style harkens back to the Jewish Golden Age in Spain under Muslim rule. Built around 1870, Central Synagogue is one of the area's oldest continuously operating synagogues.

Like many major temples, it originated in the Lower East Side. Also, like other temples such as Temple Emanu-El, it is the result of two major congregations merging: Shaaray Hashomayim and Ahawath Chesed.[22]

The building was designed to resemble a famous synagogue in Budapest, Hungary. Though visually pleasing to some, in its day the unusual Moorish style was controversial. Some stakeholders worried that the imposing structure would overshadow its mission. Yet, the architecture endured over the decades. In 1975, it was designated a National Historic Landmark.[23]

In 1998, the historic synagogue was almost destroyed in an

Central Synagogue was built in 1872. A major fire damaged it in 1998, but the building has been completely restored. (Photograph by Jessica Siemens.)

accidental fire, though there were no serious injuries. To the great relief of the congregants, the ark was miraculously spared. Thanks to the heroic efforts of a fireman, remnants of the stained glass were saved, which meant replacements could be made. The restoration was completed in 2001.

The temple credits the Eighth Battalion of the New York City Fire Department for "saving the skeleton of the building and many of the windows and walls." Ironically, the newly restored Central Synagogue was re-consecrated on September 9, 2001, just two days before the 9/11 terrorist attacks.

Tip for the Visitor: Free sanctuary tours are offered each Wednesday at 12:45 p.m. Reservations are not needed.

Eateries

Abigael's (Kosher)
1407 Broadway (at Thirty-Eighth Street)
Telephone: (212) 575-1407
Web site: www.abigaels.com
Prices: Expensive
Subway: N, Q, or R train to Times Square

This upscale kosher restaurant in the Garment District features sushi and Asian fusion cuisine. Signature dishes include boneless rib-ye steak and cashew-crusted sea bass.

Azuri Café (Kosher)
465 West Fifty-First Street (at Ninth Avenue)
Telephone: (212) 262-2920
Web site: www.azuricafe.com
Prices: Inexpensive
Subway: 1 train to Fiftieth Street

This informal, Israeli eatery has Mediterranean fare: stuffed grape leaves, shawarma gyros, and chicken shish kebabs.

Kosher beef salamis in window of local deli. (Photograph by Jessica Siemens.)

Ben's Kosher Delicatessen Restaurants & Caterers

209 West Thirty-Eighth Street (between Seventh and Eighth
   avenues)
Telephone: (212) 398-2367
Web site: www.bensdeli.net
Prices: Moderate
Subway: 1, 2, 3, N, Q, or R train to Forty-Second Street

Since 1972, Ben's has been offering kosher deli fare in the Garment
District. Diners give positive reviews on the matzo ball soup,
pickles, coleslaw, and stuffed cabbage.

Carnegie Deli

854 Seventh Avenue (between Fifty-Fourth and Fifty-Fifth
   streets)
Telephone: (800) 334-5606
Web site: www.carnegiedeli.com
Prices: Moderate
Subway: A, C, B, D, or 1 train to Fifty-Ninth Street/Columbus
   Circle; or N, Q, or R train to Fifty-Seventh Street/Seventh
   Avenue; or B, D, or E train to Seventh Avenue; or F train to
   Fifty-Seventh Street/Sixth Avenue

You may recognize the lettering on the iconic sign outside this restaurant. Or perhaps you remember the deli in scenes from Woody Allen's hit film *Broadway Danny Rose*. One of the oldest continuously operating delis in the country, Carnegie Deli stands apart from the rest for its seventy-five-year-plus history, its curing and smoking of meat in its own factory, and its world-famous cheesecake.

The deli serves prodigious portions of pastrami, corned beef, and other meats in addition to traditional Eastern European Jewish dishes such as smoked salmon, matzo ball soup, and potato pancakes. The well-known eatery also offers non-kosher items such as ham, sausage, and bacon. The restaurant's motto is: "If you can finish your meal, we've done something wrong." Diners should expect impertinent service, often a characteristic of New York delis. Menu selections are named after celebrated customers. Broadway themes and Yiddish words can also be found, with dishes such as "the egg and oy" (*The Egg and I*). Read the menu closely and look for the word plays. Try the "50 Ways to Love Your Liver," named after the Paul Simon song "50 Ways to Leave Your Lover." Owner Milton Parker passed away in 2009. He

Carnegie Deli was featured in Woody Allen's hit film Broadway Danny Rose.

wrote a book with Allyn Freeman called *How to Feed Friends and Influence People: The Carnegie Deli,* showcasing the iconic deli's history. Inquire at the cash register about purchasing the book.[24]

Le Marais (Kosher)

150 West Forty-Sixth Street (between Sixth and Seventh
  avenues)
Telephone: (212) 869-0900
Web site: www.lemarais.net
Prices: Moderate

Located in the Theater District, Le Marais is popular for its steaks. Signature dishes are the prime rib and merguez, spicy lamb sausages. Salads include artichoke hearts and portobello mushrooms.

Pongal (Kosher)

110 Lexington Avenue (between Twenty-Seventh and Twenty-
  Eighth streets)
Telephone: (212) 696-9458
Web site: www.pongalnyc.com
Prices: Moderate

This restaurant serves vegetarian Indian food, specializing in Utthappam and dosai. Try the sambar, the traditional lentil and vegetable soup.

The Prime Grill (Kosher)

25 West Fifty-Sixth Street (between Fifth and Sixth
  avenues); also Prime KO at 217 West Eighty-Fifth Street
Telephone: (212) 692-9292
Web site: www.theprimegrill.com
Prices: Expensive

This award-winning kosher steakhouse offers cuts from its private dry-aging room, such as a Prime Grill filet and prime New York rib. Non-beef selections include miso baked Chilean sea bass and Long Island breast of duck. The famed steakhouse was founded in

2000 by Joey Allaham, a fourth-generation butcher from Syria. He and Executive Chef David Kolotkin wrote *The Prime Grill Cookbook*, published by Pelican. The Prime Grill has been voted New York's number-one kosher restaurant by Zagat over the last several years.

2nd Avenue Deli (Kosher)
162 East Thirty-Third Street (between Lexington and Third
  avenues)
Telephone: (212) 689-9000
Web site: www.2ndavedeli.com
Prices: Moderate
Subway: 6 train to Thirty-Third Street

This iconic deli symbolizes both the hope and tragedy of the immigrant experience. It is a must for any deli lover. There are two locations: one on Thirty-Third Street between Lexington and Third avenues and another on the Upper East Side on Seventy-Fifth Street between First and York avenues. At either location, consider trying some of the popular dishes: stuffed cabbage, gefilte fish, stuffed derma, chopped liver, Hungarian beef goulash, "franks in blankets," smoked salmon tartare, split pea soup, turkey gumbo, and the matzo ball soup, which is often described as "Jewish penicillin."

Background

The deli began with "Uncle Abie," as he is referred to. Upon arriving in America, Uncle Abie worked at a deli in Coney Island as a soda jerk. Later he was promoted to counterman, which was considered a large step up. Like many other future deli owners, Uncle Abie worked in several deli kitchens, learning the ins and outs of traditional Jewish fare.

Abe transitioned from employee to entrepreneur in 1954. He purchased a ten-seat luncheonette on East Tenth Street at Second Avenue, the future location and name of the deli.[25] Like Sylvia's in Harlem, the small eatery became an international destination.

More than four decades later, tragedy struck. On March 4, 1996, while on his way to the bank to make a deposit, Abe was killed. Partially as a tribute to the fallen founder, Abe's widow Eleanor, daughter Sharon, and brother Jack kept the famed deli running for ten years at the namesake location. But in January 2006, a long-simmering dispute with the landlord over back rent and future rent hikes resulted in its closing.

The deli once again found a new life. Nephews Josh and Jeremy reopened the 2nd Avenue Deli at its current location in Murray Hill and a second location on the Upper East Side.

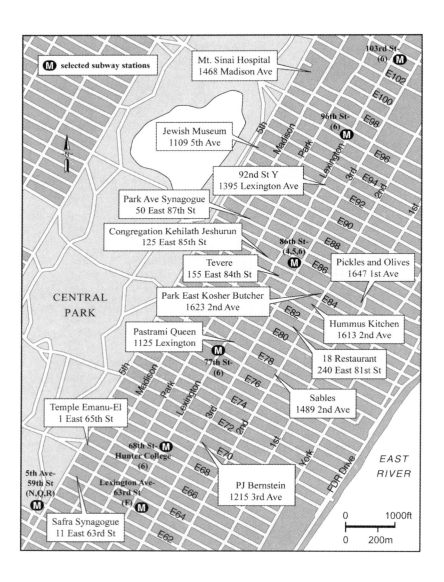

M selected subway stations

Mt. Sinai Hospital
1468 Madison Ave

Jewish Museum
1109 5th Ave

92nd St Y
1395 Lexington Ave

Park Ave Synagogue
50 East 87th St

Congregation Kehilath Jeshurun
125 East 85th St

Tevere
155 East 84th St

Pickles and Olives
1647 1st Ave

Park East Kosher Butcher
1623 2nd Ave

Hummus Kitchen
1613 2nd Ave

Pastrami Queen
1125 Lexington

18 Restaurant
240 East 81st St

Sables
1489 2nd Ave

Temple Emanu-El
1 East 65th St

PJ Bernstein
1215 3rd Ave

Safra Synagogue
11 East 63rd St

103rd St-
(6)

96th St-
(6)

86th St-
(4,5,6)

77th St-
(6)

68th St-
Hunter College
(6)

5th Ave-
59th St
(N,Q,R)

Lexington Ave-
63rd St
(F)

CENTRAL
PARK

EAST
RIVER

5th
Madison
Park
Lexington
3rd
2nd
1st
York
FDR Drive

E102
E100
E98
E96
E94
E92
E90
E88
E86
E84
E82
E80
E78
E76
E74
E72
E70
E68
E66
E64
E62

0   1000ft
0   200m

Upper East Side

Visit iconic synagogues of the Reform movement, such as Temple Emanu-El. View the latest art exhibits at the Jewish Museum, located in a former mansion. Attend a lecture by a famous personality at the most famous Young Men's Hebrew Association (YMHA) in the world. Though the Upper East Side is less known for Jewish fare than the Lower East Side, there are a number of options. One of the city's best pastrami shops and the iconic 2nd Avenue Deli are but two examples.

Museums

Jewish Museum

1109 Fifth Avenue (on Ninety-Second Street between Fifth and
    Madison avenues)
Open Thursday-Tuesday 11 a.m.–5:45 p.m. (Thursday till 8 p.m.)
Admission: $12 for adults, $7.50 for students, $10 for seniors,
    Saturdays free
Telephone: (212) 423-3200
Web site: www.thejewishmuseum.org
Subway: 6 train to Ninety-Sixth Street

Walking past the historic buildings on Ninety-Second Street between Fifth and Madison, you will stumble upon one of the largest Jewish museums in the world. Housed in a former mansion, it offers a permanent collection of Jewish artifacts, rotating exhibits on Jewish artists or entertainers, and public programming of lectures by key thinkers.

    As you enter the museum, see what temporary exhibit is featured. Many focus on well-known artists but present a different angle from what you may have seen at other museums. For example, the museum presented an exhibit on Marc Chagall that examined the effects of World War II and personal strife on his art. It also explored his representation of religion. As you peruse the museum, notice the remnants of its residential past in the details of the room. The candelabras, fireplace, and decorative moldings harken back to its pre-museum days.

The permanent exhibit showcases artifacts and ritual objects from Ashkanzi, Sephardic, and Mizrahi (Middle Eastern origin) peoples. View parts of a wall from an Iranian temple, Hanukkah candles from around the world, and artifacts and remnants from local Jewish communities.

Be sure to check the list of Public Programs for lectures and panels on subjects such as art, architecture, and the works of Karl Marx and Sigmund Freud.

If you crave a light snack while at the museum, try the downstairs Café Weissman, which serves pastries, bagels and lox, soup, sandwiches, and salads. Lox at Café Weissman is certified kosher by National Kosher Supervision. The items are expensive, though.

Background

The famed museum was established in 1904 in the Jewish Theological Seminary of America library near Columbia University. Four decades later, it moved to its current location on Fifth Avenue in the Warburg House.[1]

Felix Warburg, who prospered in the investment banking industry, married Frieda Schiff, the daughter of the chief executive of his company. Years later, in 1944, she donated the mansion to the museum.[2]

Tip for the Visitor: Take a forty-five-minute tour led by trained docents. Check the website for details. Also, take advantage of the free audio tours. When you are on the go, learn about a current exhibit at the Web site or use museum apps on your iPhone or Android. Some apps are free, while others range between $.99 and $1.99 per download.

Places of Interest

Judaica Classics by Doina
Lexington Avenue between Eighty-Fourth and Eighty-Fifth
  Street
Telephone: (212) 722-4271
Web site: www.judaicaclassics.com
Subway: 4, 5, or 6 train to Eighty-Sixth Street

At this shop, browse the unique collections of menorahs, ketubahs, Seder plates, and religious books. If you are interested in personalizing any of the objects, ask about the engraving services.

Mount Sinai Hospital
Fifth Avenue between 98th and 101st streets
Web site: www.mountsinai.org
Subway: 6 train to Ninety-Sixth Street

Like many charities, this hospital started with a vision—free medical care for poor Jews. That dream became a reality in 1855, when, on West Twenty-Eighth Street, a remote part of the growing city, the forty-five-bed Jews' Hospital was born.

Jews' Hospital admitted patients of any religious affiliation. Many of its early patients were foreign born. A few years later, during the Civil War, the hospital expanded to treat wounded Union soldiers. It also provided soldiers, as many physicians and other staff were drafted or volunteered for the war effort.

Jews' Hospital changed its sectarian charter to receive government aid in 1866. It became "Mount Sinai Hospital." Six years later, it relocated to a larger facility on Lexington Avenue between Sixty-Sixth and Sixty-Seventh streets.[3]

In the early 1930s, the hospital provided a professional home for physicians fleeing Nazi Germany. Many of these led a group that helped establish Mount Sinai Medical School in 1963. During World War II, when large numbers of nurses were serving abroad, the hospital ramped up its training of new nurses to fill the shortage at home. Pres. Franklin D. Roosevelt appointed the president of the Mount Sinai Medical Board to serve as chief medical director for the Office of Civilian Defense.

Today, Mount Sinai Hospital is renowned worldwide for its research. As one example, it was the first medical institution to link cigarettes and asbestos to cancer.

Ninety-Second Street Young Men's Hebrew Association (YMHA) Performing Arts Center

1395 Lexington Avenue (between Ninety-Second and Ninety-Third streets)

Telephone: (212) 415-5729

Web site: www.92y.org

Subway: 4, 5, or 6 train to Eighty-Sixth Street

On busy Lexington Avenue, you will enter the most famous YMHA in the nation. It is the oldest and largest in the U.S. still in continuous use. It also is one of the only ones to offer dormitories. Whether you live in the area or are just visiting, take advantage of its world-class resources. Use the famed facility to find a new passion. Discover poetry. Hear lectures from celebrities, heads of state, and noted journalists. Try creative writing. Sign up for a neighborhood tour. Or get in a great workout.

If you like literature, then be sure to explore the Unterberg Poetry Center, which has hosted notable poets such as Dylan Thomas, Allen Ginsberg, and E. E. Cummings.[4] Listen to a poetry reading or, better yet, submit your waiting-to-be-discovered poem to the *Discovery/Boston Review*.

The speakers at the YMHA are some of the most famous in the world. Check the current list of lectures on the Web site.

The YMHA also offers workout facilities, gym classes, and educational/art classes.[5] If you are interested in a membership, take a tour of its vast twin buildings.

Historic Synagogues

Temple Emanu-El (Reform)
One East Sixty-Fifth Street (between Fifth and Madison
    avenues)
Open Sunday-Thursday 10 a.m.–4:30 p.m., Saturday 1 p.m.–4:30
    p.m.
Free admission
Telephone: (212) 744-1400
Web site: www.emanuelnyc.org
Subway: 6 train to Sixty-Eighth Street; or N, Q, or R train to
    Fifth Avenue/Fifty-Ninth Street

Its cathedral-like structure stands prominently on Fifth Avenue.
During a service, the organ music resonates around the magnificent
sanctuary. The choir sings. The stained glass on the surrounding
walls and the vastness of the sanctuary create a sacred space.
Attend a service, if possible, and listen to the majestic singing.
Revel in the tranquility of the sanctuary.

Background

   Temple Emanu-El is one of the most magnificent synagogues
in the world, but like many synagogues in New York, it grew
from humble origins. In 1845, thirty-three German Jews started
the congregation in a loft on the Lower East Side's Grand and
Clinton streets. At the time, the Lower East Side had such a high
concentration of Germans that it was called *Klein Deutschland*, or
"Little Germany." Many were already moving uptown in search
of more space and quiet. In the mid-nineteenth century, some
synagogues were acquiring former churches. Temple Emanu-El
followed this trend, and in October 1847, the congregation moved
to a Methodist church located at 56 Chrystie Street.

   Though its history paralleled that of many other synagogues,
its rituals differed. In establishing "classical" Reform Judaism,
the congregation adopted major changes. German, the language
of many of its congregants, took the place of Hebrew in prayers.
Music was played during services; formerly, any type of music was
prohibited on Shabbat.

Exterior of the magnificent Temple Emanu-El, one of the oldest congregations in America, established in 1845. The congregation has worshipped in this location since 1929. (Photograph by Jessica Siemens.)

A few years later, the growing congregation moved the temple to Twelfth Street. More controversial changes followed. Departing from the segregation of genders, men and women sat together. The observance of key holidays was shortened from the usual two days to one.

After the Civil War, the synagogue moved yet again. In 1868, Emanu-El built a new place of worship in Moorish Revival, a popular style, at the corner of Forty-Third Street and Fifth Avenue. Departures from other rituals continued. Men prayed without covering their heads.

The congregation merged with Temple Beth-El in 1927. Then in 1929, the merged congregation moved from what was a highly commercialized area to its current site in the residential neighborhood at Sixty-Fifth Street and Fifth Avenue.

The congregants were mostly German, affluent, and assimilated, with liberal interpretations of ritual. They embraced the budding classical Reform movement.

Differing ritual practices and demographics created a cultural gulf between the congregation and the more pious and often poorer Eastern European Jews downtown. Each group had misgivings about the other. This shifted slightly in the 1930s and 1940s when the temple accepted poor Eastern European immigrant families. Many of these came from Yiddish-speaking and Orthodox backgrounds. For many, joining the established temple was a social step up. This incoming population in turn affected the existing congregation.[6]

Tips for the Visitor: Temple Emanu-El is home to world's largest synagogue organ, with over ten thousand pipes, some as short as a pen with others over thirty feet tall.[7]

Notable members of Temple Emanu-El have included Oscar S. Straus, Louis Marshall, Joan Rivers, and Michael Bloomberg.

First visit the elaborate and awe-inspiring sanctuary. Take the self-guided tour by entering through the Marvin and Elisabeth Cassell Community House (One East Sixty-Fifth Street).

Then visit the Bernard Museum of Congregation Emanu-El of New York, located on the Community House's second floor. The museum holds more than 650 pieces, dating back to the fourteenth century. It showcases treasures both from Temple Emanu-El's history and from Jewish communities around the globe, demonstrating the adaptability of Jewish culture in different settings.

If you are with a group of more than ten, you can pre-book a forty-five-minute tour of the sanctuary or a thirty-minute tour of the museum, or both.

Also, if you are a resident or will be staying for over a month in the New York area, then consider enrolling in a noncredit class at the adjacent Skirball Center for Adult Jewish Learning at Temple Emanu-El. The courses are excellent, with informative and engaging instructors. Student reviews are generally very positive. Course topics include history, philosophy, holidays, and literature. Most involve homework, which includes readings of primary or secondary texts. Many courses are six to eight weeks and are affordable, ranging from $200 to $800 based on their length. Learn more at www.adultjewishlearning.org.

Congregation Kehilath Jeshurun (KJ) (Orthodox)
125 East Eighty-Fifth Street
Telephone: (212) 774-5600
Web site: www.ckj.org
Subway: 4, 5, or 6 train to Eighty-Sixth Street

Following the trend established by other synagogues of the period, Congregation Kehilath Jeshurun (KJ or CKJ) was founded in 1872 by Eastern European Jewish immigrants on the Lower East Side and then later moved uptown. The congregation has suffered setbacks over the last few years. In January 2009, the *New York Times* reported that the congregation lost $3.5 million in the Bernard Madoff scandal.[8] Three years later, a fire roared throughout the upper floors of the 110-year-old building. The roof collapsed. No one was killed, but five firefighters were injured.[9]

Park Avenue Synagogue (Conservative)
50 East Eighty-Seventh Street (between Madison and Fifth
    avenues)
Telephone: (212) 369-2600
Web site: www.pasyn.org
Subway: 4, 5, or 6 train to Eighty-Sixth Street

Founded by German and Hungarian Jews, Park Avenue Synagogue is today a flagship Conservative congregation. The congregation began in 1882 against the backdrop of two trends of the time: German-Jewish congregations moving uptown, and the adoption of classical Reform Judaism. Founded as the "Temple Gates of Hope," the synagogue merged several times and changed its name to Agudat Yesharim, or the "Association of the Righteous." Services were considered Reform, with sermons in German. The place of worship was referred to as the "Eighty-Sixth Street Temple." In the 1920s, the temple formally asked the state of New York to change its name to the "Park Avenue Synagogue." Three years later, a new sanctuary was built on Eighty-Seventh Street, the current location, with Moorish architecture.

During World War II, its rabbi, Judah Nadich (1912-2007), was the senior Jewish chaplain for the U.S. armed forces in Europe and General Eisenhower's advisor on Jewish affairs in Germany. One of his key roles was to aid the hundreds of thousands of concentration-camp survivors who were displaced at the war's end. Around this time, the congregation transitioned from Reform to Conservative to accommodate mergers with several congregations. Today, it is considered one of the preeminent Conservative congregations in the United States.

Congregation Edmond J. Safra Synagogue (Sephardic)
11 East Sixty-Third Street (between Madison and Fifth avenues)
Telephone: (212) 754-9555
Web site: www.ejsny.org
Subway: N, Q, or R train to Fifth Avenue/Fifty-Ninth Street

Walking by the storied buildings on Sixty-Third Street between Fifth and Madison avenues, you might miss this relatively new synagogue. Unlike its Ashkenazi neighbors, the Edmond J. Safra Synagogue is a house of worship for Sephardic Jews on the Upper East Side. It opened its doors in March 2003. The congregation comprises many families from a medley of Middle Eastern backgrounds, though it is open to all.

If you can attend services, you will notice the sanctuary's seven-sided shape. The bema is in the center. As is traditional for Orthodox services, women sit in the seven-sided balcony upstairs.

Edmond J. Safra built the Republic National Bank of New York in the mid-1960s. In 1988, he established Safra Republic Holdings S.A. He died under tragic and somewhat mysterious circumstances and, by donating 50 percent of his assets to charities, left behind an enormous legacy. Some of the money was used to construct and renovate synagogues in urban, rural, and international communities.[10]

Eateries

Eighteen Restaurant (Kosher)
240 East Eighty-First Street (between Second and Third
    avenues)
Telephone: (212) 517-2400
Web site: www.eighteenrestaurant.com
Prices: Moderate
Subway: 4, 5, or 6 train to Eighty-Sixth Street

Eighteen Restaurant offers a varied menu, from burgers to sushi
(including a low-carb sushi roll). The restaurant also has extensive
menus for some Jewish holidays.

Georgettes Kitchen (Kosher)
Sixty-Fifth Street between Second and Third avenues
Telephone: (917) 238-9712
Web site: www.georgetteskitchen.com
Prices: Moderate
Subway: 6 train to Sixty-Eighth Street

Georgettes Kitchen serves primarily Moroccan-Jewish food, including Moroccan omelets, fried whitefish in light Moroccan sauce, gold-
en raisin and apricot chicken, sweet couscous, and Dafina-Moroccan
cholent, which includes potatoes, chickpeas, barley, rice, and meat.

Hummus Kitchen (Kosher)
1613 Second Avenue (between Eighty-Third and Eighty-Fourth
    streets)
Telephone: (212) 988-0090
Web site: www.hummuskitchen.com
Prices: Moderate
Subway: 4, 5, or 6 train to Eighty-Sixth Street

Hummus Kitchen specializes in kosher Mediterranean food and
is best known for its flavorful, protein-rich hummus made with
organic chickpeas. Try the Moroccan wrap, the super healthy

salad of quinoa, apricots, cranberries, and walnuts, or the Mediterranean red chicken.

Pastrami Queen (Kosher)
1125 Lexington Avenue (between Seventy-Eighth and Seventy-Ninth streets)
Telephone: (212) 734-1500
Web site: www.pastramiqueen.com
Prices: Moderate
Subway: 6 train to Seventy-Seventh Street

Some New Yorkers claim that this is one of the best places in the city for pastrami. Many customers opt for the overstuffed pastrami sandwich. Sandwich sizes are colossal, ranging from "overstuffed" to "royal size" to "triple decker." Try the noodle pudding for dessert.

PJ Bernstein
1215 Third Avenue (between Seventieth and Seventy-First streets)
Telephone: (212) 879-0914
Web site: www.pjbernstein.com
Prices: Moderate
Subway: 6 train to Sixty-Eighth Street

PJ Bernstein is a traditional Jewish deli. Patrons recommend the chopped chicken liver, cold borscht with boiled potato, potato pancakes, and homemade meat and potato pierogis, all made from the deli's own recipes. Online reviews rave about the matzo ball soup.

Sables Smoked Fish
1489 Second Avenue (between Seventy-Seventh and Seventy-Eighth streets)
Telephone: (212) 249-6177
Web site: www.sablesnyc.com
Prices: Moderate
Subway: 6 train to Seventy-Seventh Street

This is a must-visit for any smoked-fish lovers. The restaurant is broken into two parts. The first sells a variety of some of the city's best smoked fish as takeout. The other part is a sit-down restaurant where you order at the counter.

Sables is known for its variety of smoked salmon, including Irish and Gravlax, not to mention the whitefish, lobster, or shrimp salads. In the restaurant section, it offers a lunch special consisting of a pastrami or corned beef sandwich, pickle, and matzo ball soup. Ask for samples of the various smoked fish.

2nd Avenue Deli (Kosher)

1442 First Avenue (at Seventy-Fifth Street)
Telephone: (212) 737-1700
Web site: www.2ndavedeli.com
Prices: Moderate
Subway: 6 train to Seventy-Seventh Street

This is the Upper East Side branch of the East Thirty-Third Street deli. For background about this notable deli, including the backstory of the family who owns it, see the "Chelsea and Midtown" chapter.

Tal Bagels

333 East Eighty-Sixth Street (between Second and First
    avenues)
Telephone: (212) 427-6811
Web site: www.talbagels.com
Prices: Moderate
Subway: 4, 5, or 6 train to Eighty-Sixth Street

If you are craving a traditional bagel-and-lox place, you have found it at Tal. Offerings include a variety of fish spreads for bagels, such as nova, sable, chopped herring, and baked salmon. Also, Tal serves homemade soups and quiches.

Tevere (Kosher)
155 East Eighty-Fourth Street (between Lexington and Third
   avenues)
Telephone: (212) 744-0210
Web site: www.teverenyc.com
Prices: Moderate
Subway: 4, 5, or 6 train to Eighty-Sixth Street

This premier kosher establishment is known for its artichokes
served "Roman Jewish style" and its "Grigliata Romana"—
various meats flavored with garlic and rosemary. The mood is
quiet and intimate.

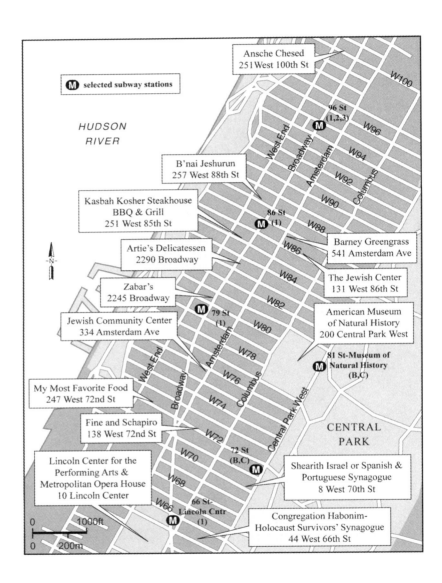

Ansche Chesed
251 West 100th St

M selected subway stations

HUDSON
RIVER

96 St
(1,2,3)

W100

W96

W94

W92

W90

West End

Broadway

Amsterdam

Columbus

B'nai Jeshurun
257 West 88th St

Kasbah Kosher Steakhouse
BBQ & Grill
251 West 85th St

86 St
(1)

W88

W86

Barney Greengrass
541 Amsterdam Ave

Artie's Delicatessen
2290 Broadway

W84

The Jewish Center
131 West 86th St

-N-

Zabar's
2245 Broadway

W82

79 St
(1)

W80

American Museum
of Natural History
200 Central Park West

Jewish Community Center
334 Amsterdam Ave

Amsterdam

W78

81 St-Museum of
Natural History
(B,C)

W76

Columbus

My Most Favorite Food
247 West 72nd St

West End

Broadway

W74

Central Park West

Fine and Schapiro
138 West 72nd St

W72

72 St
(B,C)

CENTRAL
PARK

Lincoln Center for the
Performing Arts &
Metropolitan Opera House
10 Lincoln Center

W70

W68

Shearith Israel or Spanish &
Portuguese Synagogue
8 West 70th St

W66

66 St-
Lincoln Cntr
(1)

Congregation Habonim-
Holocaust Survivors' Synagogue
44 West 66th St

0   1000ft
0   200m

Upper West Side

This neighborhood is home to a vibrant Jewish community of all affiliations. Stroll through the area and see the current locations of some of the country's oldest congregations. Shop Judaica stores and sample the culinary delights of the local delis.

Martin Shore, a historian and tour guide of Jewish Manhattan, notes that at the turn of the twentieth century, the Jewish population in the Upper West Side was small, aside from some wealthy Jews around Central Park. Then in the 1920s, middle-class Jews started to move into the neighborhood, facilitated by the opening of the subway, which provided easy access to their jobs. Many moved from Harlem.

From the 1920s to the late 1950s, the Jewish Upper West Side grew, only to decline in the 1960s. Many synagogues were struggling by the 1970s, as their congregations aged and dwindled and the neighborhood experienced an increasing crime rate. By the mid-1980s, economic conditions improved, leading to a gentrification of the Upper West Side. The Jewish population was revitalized, and today it is thriving. On any Friday night or Saturday, you will see scores of families or individuals on their way to synagogue services.

Museums and Performance Venues

Lincoln Center for the Performing Arts and Metropolitan Opera House
Broadway and Sixty-Third Street
Telephone: (212) 721-6500
Web site: www.lincolncenter.org
Subway: 1 train to Sixty-Sixth Street; or 2 or 3 to Fifty-Ninth Street

Lincoln Center consists primarily of the following institutions:

- Metropolitan Opera House
- David Koch Theater
- Avery Fisher Hall
- Vivian Beaumont Theater
- Alice Tully Hall
- Julliard School of Music
- Museum of the Performing Arts

The Metropolitan Opera House was first located at 1423 Broadway, between Thirty-Ninth and Fortieth streets. It moved to its present-day location at Lincoln Center in 1966, opening with *Antony and Cleopatra.*[1]

The genesis of Lincoln Center is not only a story about great performances but also urban renewal. Prior to Lincoln Center's construction, the neighborhood was rundown and condemned. The site was used in the filming of Leonard Bernstein's classic, *West Side Story.* Bernstein was a famous Jewish composer, author, and conductor. According to the *New York Times,* he was "one of the most prodigiously talented and successful musicians in American history." His fame derived from his long tenure as the music director of the New York Philharmonic, his conducting most of the world's leading orchestras, his music for *West Side Story, Candide, Wonderful Town,* and *On the Town,* and his classical compositions."[2]

Another Jewish connection may be found in the grand lobby of the Metropolitan Opera House, which contains two colorful thirty-by-thirty-six-foot paintings by Marc Chagall, the celebrated Jewish artist of Russian and French descent. The two giant murals, *Triumph of Music* and *Sources of Music,* were painted in the mid-1960s. Stand in the plaza outside the opera house and admire the unique works.

Robert Hughes, a noted art critic, referred to Chagall as "the quintessential Jewish artist of the twentieth century." He produced stained-glass windows for some of the world's most notable structures: the cathedrals of Reims and Metz, the windows for the UN, and the Jerusalem Windows in Israel. He was particularly renowned for his use of color. "When Matisse dies," legendary artist Pablo Picasso said in the 1950s, "Chagall will be the only painter left who understands what color really is."[3] The Jewish Museum (see "Upper East Side" chapter) ran a prominent exhibit on the Russian artist in 2013-14. It revealed how both world and personal conflicts influenced the imagery in his post-World War II work.[4]

If you like watching opera, catch a performance at the majestic, multilevel Metropolitan Opera. Part of the fun is looking at the ornate sets and elaborate costumes. Though most of the operas are not in English, there are electronic subtitles to guide you. If you are on a budget, go for the $20 rush tickets for weekday performances. Try the box office about two hours before the performance. The seats are often good, but make sure you know exactly what seat level you are buying. There are also student discounts ranging from $25 to $35.[5]

Tip for the Visitor: Go on the "Behind the Scenes Look" backstage tour at the Metropolitan Opera. You will learn about the operations behind one of the world's largest performance venues. You may get to view the costume room and the set design, and you will better understand many of the pieces that must come together for a seamless performance. Tour tickets are $20. Another option is to tour Lincoln Center. This should be plan B, though, as you do not get to see as much backstage. Tickets are $15.[6]

American Museum of Natural History
200 Central Park West (between Seventy-Seventh and Eighty-
   First streets)
Telephone: (212) 769-5100
Web site: www.amnh.org
Subway: B or C train to Eighty-First Street

This museum is considered one of the best natural history museums in the world and is worth a thorough visit in its own right. The

Jewish connection lies in the permanent exhibition of Asian peoples on the second floor. The display contains information about the culture, history, and artifacts of Asian Jewish communities in Turkey, India, Yemen, Iraq, and Iran. The exhibit also contains Jewish ceremonial and folk-art objects from the sixth through nineteenth centuries, including a silver Torah case. As the West is less familiar with these Jewish communities, the exhibition is fascinating.

Places of Interest

Jewish Community Center of the Upper West Side
334 Amsterdam Avenue (at Seventy-Sixth Street)
Telephone: (646) 505-4444
Web site: www.jccmanhattan.org
Subway: 1, 2, 3, B, or C train to Seventy-Second Street

There are many Jewish community centers around the world. But this one is impressive for the size and breadth of its offerings. As you enter, view the public art exhibition on the first floor. Sometimes local artists exhibit; other times it presents a theme. A small café stands in the corner overlooking Amsterdam Avenue for people to relax and watch the street. If the staff allows you to explore the center, or if you are a member, visit the roof for a spectacular view of the Upper West Side. Check the calendar for celebrations on the rooftop. During the holiday of Succot, for example, there is a Succah.

The beauty of the JCC is how it allows you to explore activities you either never tried or never knew existed. Have you attempted Jewish meditation? What about cooking classes, such as "Early Autumn Soups and Salads"? Any interest in printmaking?

In terms of programming, the center offers "Adaptions—the Young Adult Life Skills Network," which addresses special needs. Some meditation classes teach students how to reduce stress and increase focus. Others also present unique approaches to religious practices, such as sound prayer, utilizing vocal tones based on the "ancient Jewish understanding of the Tree of Life."[7] The film programming is also outstanding. Look for any film festivals going on, such as the famed Israeli film series, the series on children with special needs, and much more.

Traditional community-center offerings include a health and fitness club; programs for youth, adults, and senior citizens; Shabbat dinners; and educational programs.[8]

The JCC welcomes members of all backgrounds, religions, and ethnic groups.

Zabar's

2245 Broadway (at Eightieth Street)
Telephone: (212) 496-1234
Web site: www.zabars.com
Prices: Moderate
Subway: 1 train to Seventy-Ninth Street

Zabar's is a specialty food store that is not to be missed. Even if you are not planning to buy anything, the store is still worth visiting for the unique New York City experience. Browse the store without a shopping list. Try the samples and gaze at the variety of smoked fish, salamis, and cheeses. Listen for announcements for daily goodies such as smoked mussels from Maine.

Louis Zabar was a 1920s immigrant who fled political persecution in the Ukraine. His father was killed in a pogrom. Like many famous entrepreneurs, Zabar started small, renting a modest stall within a farmer's market. He specialized in smoked fish—food reminiscent of his Eastern European background. In search of the best supplier, he visited smokehouses to sample the smoked fish himself. As his business prospered, he and his wife expanded their operations.[9] He acquired about ten more markets before his death in 1950. For the next several decades, his sons, Saul and Stanley, partnered with entrepreneur Murray Klein to continue the business. Under their direction, the regional deli became an internationally recognized culinary brand. Saul and Stanley still manage the business,[10] while other family members run the mail-order business.

Historic Synagogues

Ansche Chesed (Conservative)
251 West 100th Street (between Broadway and West End
   Avenue)
Telephone: (212) 865-0600
Web site: www.anschechesed.org
Subway: 1 train to 103rd Street; or 1, 2, or 3 to Ninety-Sixth
   Street

Ansche Chesed is one of the city's oldest congregations still
operating. It was founded in 1828 by German, Dutch, and Polish
Jews who left Congregation B'nai Jeshurun. The precise reasons
for their departure are unknown, but such splits were somewhat
commonplace in that period. In 1850, the congregation erected
its first building on Norfolk Street on the Lower East Side, in the
structure now called Angel Orensanz Center (see "Lower East Side"
chapter for more information on the Angel Orensanz temple).

The growing German Jewish congregation moved uptown,
occupying various buildings, including one on Grand Street, and
ultimately settling in the Upper East Side. In 1908, when Harlem
had many synagogues, the blossoming congregation relocated
to a neoclassical temple at 114th Street and what is now Adam
Clayton Powell Jr. Boulevard.

As Jews started moving out of Harlem and into the Upper West
Side in the 1920s (see "Harlem and Morningside Heights" chapter
for details), Ansche Chesed followed. In 1927, the cornerstone was
laid at its current location at 100th Street and West End Avenue.

Economic booms and busts in the city would follow, impacting
the congregation. The 1929 stock-market crash halted expansion
and hurt many members financially. But in the decades following
the Great Depression, the temple bounced back. The tide would
turn again in the late 1960s and 1970s, when Jewish middle-class
families started to leave the city for the suburbs, and Ansche
Chesed's membership plummeted. It was under dire financial
stress, as was the entire city. In the 1980s, the situation turned
around yet again as families started moving back into the

neighborhood. The trend accelerated in the 1990s and 2000s during a new gentrification process. The congregation revived.

B'nai Jeshurun (Independent, associated with Conservative)

257 West Eighty-Eighth Street (between Broadway and West
   End Avenue)
Web site: www.bj.org
Subway: 1 train to Eighty-Sixth Street

B'nai Jeshurun is the oldest Ashkenazic congregation in North America. It broke away from Shearith Israel (also known as the Spanish and Portuguese Synagogue) in 1825. This synagogue has a service like no other you have likely seen. The lively Shabbat services are known for the instrumental accompaniment, enchanting melodies, "Broadway voice" caliber of the cantor, and compelling sermons that seem to resonate with contemporary congregations. On a Friday night, the energy is high as congregants dance in the aisles to welcome the "Shabbat queen." The tunes are hypnotic. On the Web site, you can hear some of the beautiful songs spanning centuries and continents, including Sephardic and Ashkenazic melodies.[11]

Background

   B'nai Jeshurun's dynamic history began with its separation from Shearith Israel (the Spanish and Portuguese Synagogue). The congregation's stated intention was to follow the "German and Polish *minhag*" (rite). Its first building was on Elm Street. In 1828, some of its congregants broke away yet again and formed Ansche Chesed. In the mid-nineteenth century, the growing congregation needed more space. It built on Green Street.

   In 1865, the congregation moved a third time, to a building on Thirty-Fourth Street. The area was more remote than the previous location but within a few decades became more commercialized. Twenty years later, the congregation moved again, to the Upper East Side on Madison Avenue at Sixty-Fifth Street.

   In 1917, as Jews started moving from Harlem into the Upper West Side, the congregation relocated once more. It finally settled at its current site on West Eighty-Eighth Street between Broadway and West End Avenue.

The famed B'nai Jeshurun is known for its lively musical Shabbat services.
(Photograph by Jessica Siemens.)

As with many other congregations on the Upper West Side, membership plummeted as many families moved to the suburbs. But in the mid-1980s, the congregation's fortunes reversed, and interest in the historic congregation increased. Attendance spiked with the musical and liturgical innovations of Rabbi Marshall Meyer from Buenos Aires, Argentina. The synagogue became known for its catchy melodies and lively services. Though the congregation was reviving, the building needed repair. In the mid-1990s, the elaborate ceiling collapsed. The ceiling was renovated, and the congregation continues to thrive today.

Congregation Habonim (Holocaust Survivors' Synagogue) (Conservative)

44 West Sixty-Sixth Street
Telephone: (212) 787-5347
Web site: www.habonim.net
Subway: 1 train to Sixty-Sixth Street

Habonim was founded in 1939 by German refugees fleeing the Nazis, one year after *Kristallnacht*. The members wanted to recreate the settings of synagogues in Germany associated with the Reform movement. Accordingly, there is a small display in the lobby containing stone fragments from the Essen Synagogue and the Fassanenstrasse Temple in Berlin and a burned Torah parchment.

For several decades, the primarily German congregation prospered, until demand for its services started to decrease. Ironically, the decline in membership happened for the same reasons that once made Habonim successful and unique. The founders' original intention—to recreate the German Reform synagogue—did not resonate with the next generation. By the 1970s, many children of the original members had moved away or chosen to join synagogues closer to where they lived. In 1995, in an effort to reduce its deficit and stand out in a neighborhood with no Conservative congregations, Habonim switched its affiliation from Reform to Conservative. The synagogue has now turned around due to the area's gentrification and the congregation's increased emphasis on serving young families.

The Jewish Center (Orthodox)

131 West Eighty-Sixth Street (between Columbus and
 Amsterdam avenues)
Telephone: (212) 724-2700
Web site: www.jewishcenter.org
Subway: B or C train to Eighty-Sixth Street; or 1 to Eighty-
 Sixth and Broadway

Established in 1917, the Jewish Center is a modern Orthodox
flagship institution offering a variety of services and programs.
Different organizations meet or hold services here, such as the
famed Manhattan Jewish Experience (MJE).

Background

Rabbi Mordecai Kaplan, the founder of the Reconstructionist
movement, co-created the center as a deterrent to assimilation.
He envisioned a Jewish center that "would bring Jews together
. . . for social, cultural and recreational purposes in addition to
worship."[12]

While Rabbi Kaplan shared the vision of a religious center that
was also social and educational in nature, his own views diverged
markedly from Orthodoxy. The institution's leaders knew this.
But they gambled that if he did not emphasize these religious
views, the congregation would accept him. The leaders were half-
right. Kaplan did successfully start the center on West Eighty-
Sixth Street between Amsterdam and Columbus. But he also
discussed his theology, alienating some of his congregants. Three
years later, the father of the Reconstructionist movement left his
position. His replacement, Rabbi Jung, was a vocal proponent for
Orthodox Judaism, an unpopular sentiment at the time among
the population at large.

Today, the center is still fulfilling Kaplan's vision. It hosts
educational classes, youth groups, social clubs, athletic events,
and holiday celebrations.

Congregation Romemu (Renewal)

165 West 105th Street
Telephone: (212) 580-4294
Web site: www.romemu.org
Subway: 1 train to 103rd Street

Departing from traditional Jewish services, Congregation Romemu integrates "body, mind and soul in Jewish practice." The new but thriving congregation offers meditation, yoga, and chants along with the typical prayers. The music is powerful and inspires contemplation. Congregants dance. The emphasis is on internalizing the prayer, meditation, and singing for a meaningful experience.

The congregation was created in 2006 by the visionary and charismatic Rabbi David Ingber. His background is Orthodox, which gives the services an undertone of tradition in the midst of the more spiritual elements. His teacher was Rabbi Zalman Schachter-Shalomi, the father of "Jewish Renewal."

Romemu's literature notes that it strives to create "an integral & holistic prayer experience based upon the five basic freedoms:

1. Movement: Space to stretch, dance and find the natural movement of your body that opens you to prayer.
2. Voice: Safety to find many forms of voice, including singing, speaking, crying and laughing.
3. Thought: Thinking is both critical and analytical. Both spirituality and intellectual honesty flourish together.
4. Silence: Freedom to be silent, to quiet the mind and nurture the soul through time-honored contemplative practices.
5. Commitment: An invitation to commit, to be bound to a community that expects and relies upon your active participation, both as members of the congregation and as socially conscious and aware citizens of the world."[13]

The congregation started with a handful of members. In just a few years, its membership has skyrocketed to over five hundred.

Shearith Israel (The Spanish and Portuguese Synagogue) (Orthodox, Sephardic)

8 West Seventieth Street
Telephone: (212) 873-0300
Web site: www.shearithisrael.org
Subway: B or C train to Seventieth Street

Walking by the four-column façade, you may not at first notice that you are passing by the most historic congregation in the nation. Though the building is from 1897, the congregation traces its roots back to the twenty-three Jewish refugees who landed in New Amsterdam in September 1654. View the three plaques just to the right of the Central Park West entrance, which include the inscriptions "I will take unto me faithful witnesses" (Isaiah 8:2) and the "commemoration of 300 years of freedom" (this plaque, of course, was installed in 1954). Shearith Israel, often called the Spanish and Portuguese Synagogue, is the oldest Ashkenazic congregation in North America.

See if you can tour the inside. Look at the showcases of relics from the synagogue's storied past. Consider going to a service and viewing the unique interior and Sephardic rituals.

Used as a chapel for daily prayer, the "Little Synagogue" is a room near the main sanctuary that measures thirty by thirty feet and contains original furnishings. Try to view the historical relics, such as the "Pineapple Rimonim" from the original 1730 Mill Street synagogue, used as Torah adornments during Passover. View the brass Hanukkah lamp from 1730 and the Revolutionary War Torah scrolls from 1776, some of which were desecrated by British soldiers. The Omer Board also dates back to 1730 and is used to count the number of days for seven weeks between Passover and Shavuos. The main sanctuary, used on Sabbath and major holidays, contains an eye-catching ark made of Italian marble. Harkening back to its heritage, the reading platform contains original wooden floorboards from the Mill Street synagogue.

Each year in late May, the synagogue has a ceremony at the Chatham Square cemetery celebrating bygone congregants who fought in the War for Independence. (See Oldest Jewish Cemetery in the "Lower Manhattan" chapter.)

Background

According to the synagogue's history, Shearith Israel "was the only Jewish congregation in New York City from 1654 until 1825." Until 1730, the congregation met in rented quarters. Religious restrictions were imposed under the Dutch and then, although less so, under the British. The congregation had no formal building, but it did have a cemetery in 1656.

In 1730, the vagrant congregation practicing in rented quarters and homes founded its first official building, on Mill Street—today's South William Street. In 1818, partly to accommodate the congregation's growth, the building was expanded. Shearith Israel's records indicate it "provided one hundred sixty-seven seats for men and one hundred thirty-three seats for women."[14] In 1834, the synagogue moved to Crosby Street between Spring and Broom. This building used the same cornerstone that was used in the Mill Street synagogue. Then in 1860, the congregation moved to West Nineteenth Street. But many members felt that the building, although stately, was impractical due to its poor acoustics and high number of steps to climb. As congregants continued the move uptown over the subsequent decades, in 1897 the historic congregation relocated once again—for the last time—to its current location at West Seventieth Street and Central Park West. Though it is hard to imagine today, the plot had once been the site of a duck farm.

Eateries

Artie's Delicatessen
2290 Broadway (between Eighty-Second and Eighty-Third
    streets)
Telephone: (212) 579-5959
Web site: www.arties83rd.net
Prices: Moderate
Subway: 1 or 2 train to Seventy-Ninth Street or Eighty-Sixth Street

Started in the late 1990s, Artie's Delicatessen is a retro-style deli known for its overstuffed pastrami sandwiches and traditional dishes of matzo ball soup, potato knishes and pancakes, franks in blankets, and chopped liver.

Artie's is named after the late Artie Cutler, who owned seven other restaurants: Carmine's, Docks, Ollie's, Virgils, Gabriela's, Jake's, and Columbia Bagels. This was to be his last project. His intention was to "create a 1930s-style New York Jewish delicatessen." But he died before its completion.

Similar to the histories of other delis, Artie's family continued the project after this death. His wife, brother-in-law, and other partners completed the retro deli. It opened for business in the fall of 1999.[15]

In April 2010, a new owner took over, Tuvia Feldman. Feldman vowed to keep the old traditions, while adding beer and wine selections.

Barney Greengrass
541 Amsterdam Avenue (between Eighty-Sixth and Eighty-
   Seventh streets)
Telephone: (212) 724-4707
Web site: www.barneygreengrass.com
Prices: Moderate
Subway: 1 train to Eighty-Sixth Street

This local favorite is known for its "old city feel." Try the Nova Scotia salmon, baked salmon, cured gravlax, pickled herring in cream sauce, or $220 caviar with chopped eggs and onions.

Fine and Schapiro (Kosher)
138 West Seventy-Second Street
Telephone: (212) 877-2721
Web site: www.fineandschapiro.com
Prices: Moderate
Subway: B or C train to Seventy-Second Street

Fine and Schapiro is a kosher deli that has offered traditional Jewish dishes since the 1930s. Its roots date back to the first generation of Eastern European Jews in New York. Traditional favorites include smoked fish, stuffed cabbage, chicken in the pot, brisket of beef, and matzo ball soup. The large menu has over one hundred selections.

Hummus Place (Kosher)

305 Amsterdam Avenue (between Seventy-Fourth and Seventy-
Fifth streets); 109 Saint Marks Place (between First Avenue
and Avenue A); 71 Seventh Avenue South (at Bleeker Street)
Telephone: (212) 799-3335
Web site: www.hummusplace.com
Prices: Inexpensive
Subway: 1 train to Seventy-Ninth Street

This informal local chain offers multiple varieties of hummus,
including msabbaha, fava, tahini, and mushroom.

Kasbah Kosher Steakhouse BBQ & Grill

251 West Eighty-Fifth Street (between Broadway and West End
Avenue)
Telephone: (212) 496-1500
Web site: www.delikasbah.com
Prices: Moderate
Subway: 1 train to Eighty-Sixth Street

Established in 1985, the Kasbah Kosher Steakhouse is known for
its "dry aged steaks that are cut on premises and served in sizzling
cabernet wine and marrow sauce." The menu offers a good variety
of items, ranging from sushi to specialty soups such as Moroccan
beef soup to Black Angus steaks.

My Most Favorite Food (Kosher)

247 West Seventy-Second Street (between Broadway and West
End Avenue)
Telephone: (212) 580-5130
Web site: www.mymostfavorite.com
Prices: Moderate
Subway: 1 or 2 train to Seventy-Second Street

Try the ginger-soy Chilean sea bass or fettuccini Français. Treat
yourself at the bakery, which serves apricot squares, lemon-curd
sandwich cookies, and much more.

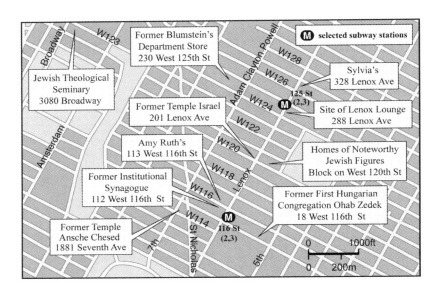

Broadway
W123
Former Blumstein's
Department Store
230 West 125th St

Adam Clayton Powell
W128
M selected subway stations

W126
Sylvia's
328 Lenox Ave

Jewish Theological
Seminary
3080 Broadway

125 St
M (2,3)

W124

Former Temple Israel
201 Lenox Ave

Site of Lenox Lounge
288 Lenox Ave

Amsterdam

W122

Amy Ruth's
113 West 116th St

W120

Homes of Noteworthy
Jewish Figures
Block on West 120th St

Lenox

W118

Former Institutional
Synagogue
112 West 116th St

W116

Former First Hungarian
Congregation Ohab Zedek
18 West 116th St

W114

M
116 St
(2,3)

7th

St Nicholas

Former Temple
Ansche Chesed
1881 Seventh Ave

5th

0   1000ft

0   200m

Harlem and Morningside Heights

Harlem is one of Jewish New York's best-kept secrets. From the 1890s to 1920s, Jews flourished in this neighborhood, and you can explore the vestiges of this life. Stroll through central Harlem and view former synagogues, such as Temple Israel and First Hungarian Congregation Ohab Zedek, both now churches. Careful observers will note traces of the buildings' past, from Stars of David to inside balconies. Walk through the childhood neighborhoods of Gertrude Edelstein, Lena Himmelstein, and Richard Rodgers. Tour the campus of the Jewish Theological Seminary, the focal point for Conservative Jewish education.

History of Jewish Harlem

Most people are not familiar with the history of Jews in Harlem. As hard as it is to imagine, in the mid-nineteenth century, Harlem was mostly farmland. In the 1890s, upper- to middle-class Jews moved to central Harlem to escape from the Lower East Side and dissociate themselves from the Eastern European, Yiddish-speaking Jewish immigrants who were flooding in. Also, the construction of the Williamsburg Bridge in the early twentieth century played a factor, as the demolition of tenements displaced many residents. A large number of them moved to Brooklyn, but quite a few came to East Harlem. Additionally, the opening of the subway in 1904 facilitated the move to Harlem.

Speculators bought up most of the land, expecting people to move away from crowded downtown conditions to new apartments in this emerging neighborhood. But a recession and housing crisis hit in 1907. According to historian Martin Shore, many of the new apartments were standing empty, prompting Philip Payton,

an African-American real-estate agent, to approach landlords
with the proposition of renting out apartments to the growing
African-American population. He argued that this move would
bring them more rent security and that they could charge above-
market rents to this population, since their options for moving
were limited. The landlords agreed, and Payton convinced many
African-Americans in various parts of the city to move to Harlem.

The heyday of Jewish Harlem lasted a few years after World
War I and then began to decline due to several factors. New laws
restricted inflows of immigrants from Southern and Eastern
Europe. Also, for Jews already in New York, more options were
available for both living and working. New apartment houses
were built in the Bronx, Brooklyn, and western Queens, with
easy subway access to Manhattan. Many Jews moved to the outer
boroughs, which were regarded as better places to raise a family
than crowded areas such as the Lower East Side. White flight was
also a factor. During the 1920s, more African-Americans moved to
Harlem. The black population increased, primarily around 135th
Street, as part of the Great Migration from the South after World
War I.

The early 1920s saw the start of the Harlem Renaissance, an
artistic and cultural movement inspired by African-Americans
who had moved to this area. As the largest African-American
neighborhood in the country, Harlem began to thrive. It became a
mecca for African-American poets, writers, musicians, and artists.
But the stock-market crash in 1929 brought an end to this period
of flourishing. Subsequently, during the depression, although some
pockets such as Striver's Row and Hamilton Heights were less
affected than others, Harlem entered a long and steep economic
decline that lasted until the 1990s.

In the late nineteenth and early twentieth centuries, most of the
shop owners on 125th Street in Harlem were Jewish. Blumstein's,
a department store, was the best known (see below), but it also
prohibited African-American women from trying on clothes in
dressing rooms. Moreover, most owners did not employ African-
Americans in the very stores they shopped in. This continued
until the 1930s, when a series of successful boycotts reversed these
discriminatory policies. But tension remained between these shop

owners and their customers, who felt, for example, that they were too closely watched by shop employees on suspicion of shoplifting.

Among the many little-known stories of Jewish Harlem, one involves an early-twentieth-century protest against increases in kosher meat prices. On May 19, 1902, protesters tied themselves to the tracks of the Third Avenue El, vowing not to untie themselves until the kosher butchers lowered their prices. As it happened, they did end up untying themselves when the train came, but it was very dramatic. Two women, Sara Elitzstein and Tina Tass, were arrested.

Places of Interest

Former Blumstein's
230 West 125th Street (between Adam Clayton Powell Jr.
  Boulevard, or Seventh Avenue, and Frederick Douglass
  Boulevard, or Eighth Avenue)
Subway: 2 or 3 train to 125th Street

Blumstein's department store embodies the story of entrepreneurship among immigrants. It also tells a story of racial discrimination and the power of protest. Louis Blumstein came to New York from Germany in the 1890s. Like many immigrants of the time, he started as a peddler and gradually expanded his trade until he opened his first store, on Hudson Street. During Harlem's growth in the late 1890s, Blumstein moved his store north. After he passed away in 1920, his family relocated the store to a five-story structure designed in an Art Nouveau and early Art Deco style, and Blumstein's became one of the major Jewish-owned department stores in New York.

The store's history also reflects the racial tensions of its time. Although many African-Americans shopped there, none was hired before 1929, and then only in certain roles, such as elevator operator or porter. A *New York Age* article noted at the time that "75% of Blumstein's sales were to African Americans but the company refused to employ them as clerks or cashiers."[1] This, in part, inspired a "Buy Where You Can Work" campaign that continued until the 1930s and was led by Adam Clayton Powell and others. The boycott was

Blumstein's was a famous department store in Harlem on 125th Street.
(Courtesy of Wally Gobetz.)

effective. William Blumstein promised to hire African-Americans for positions other than custodial work. In subsequent years, Blumstein's utilized the services of African-American Santa Clauses and models.[2]

Although the Blumstein family sold the building in 1976, the store's name still appears on its facade. The building, now owned by Touro College, houses a College of Osteopathic Medicine and a College of Pharmacy. Visitors may view the exterior only.

Lenox Lounge
288 Lenox Avenue (at 125th Street)
Web site: www.lenoxlounge.com
Subway: 2 or 3 train to 125th Street

The Lenox Lounge was known for its neon sign, A-list jazz performers, and unique décor. It also had the famed Zebra Room, named for its mixing of black and white patrons in an era when interracial socializing was taboo. The club was ahead of its time. Opening in 1939, this historic jazz venue hosted many legends, including Billie Holiday, Miles Davis, Frank Sinatra, and John Coltrane, as well as some lesser-known Jewish musicians. Literary lumaries such as Langston Hughes, James Baldwin, and Ralph Ellison were frequent customers. Alex Haley interviewed Malcolm X for his biography here; Lenox Avenue is also named Malcolm X Boulevard.[3] The Zebra Room appeared in the pilot episode of the Emmy-award-winning AMC drama *Mad Men*, titled "Smoke Gets in Your Eyes."

As the neighborhood declined in the 1970s and 1980s, so did the Lenox Lounge. When Alvin Reid, Sr., bought the faltering establishment in 1988, it no longer hosted live music. It recovered somewhat as the area became gentrified, but in December 2012, this iconic venue announced it would close due to rent increases. In 2013, the *New York Times* noted that "entrepreneur Richard Notar, who owned the Nobu Restaurant chain and who acquired the lease on the original 288 Lenox location, said he would maintain the decor of the original 288 lounge."[4] He is planning to open Notar Jazz Club here.

Reid's new Lenox Lounge is expected to open in 2015, just two blocks north. He is trying to keep the new site as close to the original as possible, including the name, signage, bar, stools, and floors.

Noteworthy Jewish Figures' Childhood Homes
120th Street between Lenox and Fifth avenues
Subway: 4, 5, or 6 train to 125th Street

Some of the "must-sees" in this area are streets with restored brownstones, such as 120th Street near Mount Morris Park, where the visitor can get a flavor of what this neighborhood was like when it was blossoming in the late nineteenth century. The houses include the childhood homes of famous Jewish figures.

Though less well known in recent decades, Gertrude Edelstein was the most significant Jewish actress and female comedian in early television. The exterior of her childhood home may be viewed here. She created *The Rise of the Goldbergs*, later known as *The Goldbergs*; she played the role of Molly. The program depicted a Jewish family persevering in the crowded New York tenements.

Gertrude Berg (her professional name) convinced CBS to put *The Goldbergs* on television in 1949. Cultural historians consider this the first situation comedy, preceding *I Love Lucy*. In some respects, the show represented the next generation of Yiddish theater, which had depicted Jewish immigrants' struggles to reach and adjust to America.

The series won critical praise but ran into political troubles during the McCarthy era. Actor Philip Loeb (who played Molly's husband, patriarch Jake Goldberg) was blacklisted. He resigned rather than cause Berg trouble and committed suicide in 1955.

For more information about this performer, see Berg's memoir, titled *Molly and Me*, and the 2009 documentary film *Yoo-Hoo, Mrs. Goldberg*.

Lena Himmelstein Bryant Malsin, the clothing designer who founded Lane Bryant, was born in 1877 in Lithuania. She lived a true rags-to-riches story. In 1895 when she joined her sister in New York, she worked in a sweatshop for one dollar per week. She became known as a talented seamstress. She lived in Harlem, first on West 112th Street and then, after 1904, on Fifth Avenue between 119th and 120th streets, where she leased space on the first floor and lived in the back with her son. A pregnant friend asked her for wardrobe advice, as suitable clothing for expecting mothers was hard to come by. From this experience she conceived the idea of a business that makes maternity clothes. She borrowed $300 to start her store, "Lane."

As Lane Bryant (her professional name), she designed and marketed the prototypical maternity dress. Her business expanded, and she opened a shop closer to the Garment District on West 38th Street.[5] Advertising was limited, because showing pregnant women was prohibited. In 1911, a rare ad appeared in the *New York Herald*.

Bryant is regarded as a pioneer in American fashion for foreseeing the need for plus-size clothing and originating the highly successful Lane Bryant brand. She also supported Jewish communal charities, including some that had probably aided in her immigration to America, such as the Hebrew Immigrant Aid Society.

Richard Rodgers, of the famous duo Rodgers and Hammerstein, grew up at 3 West 120th Street, near Mount Morris Park. The precocious musician attended nearby Columbia College and later met the famous Hammerstein II, grandson of the builder of the Harlem Opera House on 125th Street in 1889. Rodgers composed for over forty Broadway musicals, including *The King and I*, *The Sound of Music*, and *Oklahoma!*[6] He also wrote for film and TV. He is considered one of the greatest contributors to American popular music.

Jewish Theological Seminary
3080 Broadway (at 123rd Street)
Telephone: (212) 678-8000
Web site: www.jtsa.edu
Subway: 1 or 2 train to 125th Street

The Jewish Theological Seminary of America (JTS or JTSA) is one of the premier scholarly centers of the Conservative Jewish Movement. Take a tour of this storied institution, browse the rare manuscripts in its famed library, or walk through the tranquil courtyards. Check also for any lectures or programs open to the public.

JTS has five schools: Jewish Studies, Jewish Education, Cantorial School, Jewish Music, and, perhaps the most famous, Rabbinic School.[7] Some classes are open to the public, such as Hebrew Language. Inquire at the registrar's office for more information.

The library is equipped for primary research, with Bible scrolls, artifacts of Mediterranean Jewry from the second millennium, manuscripts on science and mysticism, liturgies from around the globe, and much more. For those who want to financially support the preservation of rare books and manuscripts, the library offers an annual membership for about $360. Members can borrow from the collection as well as attend the library's sponsored events.[8]

Background of the Conservative Movement

Conservative Judaism formed in reaction to what some saw as overly liberalized religious beliefs, customs, and rituals in the Reform movement. The movement sought to keep certain longstanding traditions, while modernizing others. It occupies a middle ground between Orthodox and Reform Judaism. Many, though not all, Conservative synagogues are associated with the United Synagogues of Conservative Judaism.

One of the movement's pioneers, Rabbi Zecharias Frankel, came from the Reform movement. After the second Reform rabbinic conference in 1845 in Frankfurt, Germany, he resigned to lead the Jewish Theological Seminary of Breslau. He noted that Judaism was "dynamic, changing in response to global and local conditions," a philosophy he called "Judaism Positive-Historical."[9]

Later, Solomon Schechter assumed the presidency of the new JTS. He spelled out a vision and created infrastructures for the budding Conservative movement and the United Synagogue of America, whose name subsequently changed in the early 1990s to United Synagogue of Conservative Judaism. A major change occurred in 1983 when the Rabbinic School admitted women.

Historic Synagogues

As Jews moved into Harlem from the 1890s to the 1920s, many congregations moved to the neighborhood too, and new ones were formed. Some of these synagogues became churches. In some cases, they were sold from one congregation to another. In many of these buildings, clues to their Jewish past await the careful observer. As you look at some of the buildings in this section, look carefully for a faded Star of David in the window or on top of pillars, a balcony for an Orthodox congregation, or stained glass with Jewish symbolism.

Former Temple Ansche Chesed
1881 Seventh Avenue (at 114th Street)
Subway: 2 or 3 train to 116th Street

Like many uptown temples, Ansche Chesed began in the Lower East Side, on Norfolk Street. As German Jews relocated uptown,

Former Temple Ansche Chesed building, now Mount Neboh Baptist Church. Hebrew inscriptions and tablets above the sign reveal its Jewish past. (Photograph by Jessica Siemens.)

the congregation moved to 160 East 112th Street. In 1908, it commissioned the construction of a temple at the corner of Seventh Avenue and 114th Street.

A March 8, 1908, *New York Times* article noted that the "site cost $105,000 and the building would cost $100,000."[10] Its most notable feature was a stained-glass skylight measuring about seventy-five by twenty-five feet, depicting biblical themes.

In 1927, the congregation moved to the Upper West Side to 100th Street and West End Avenue. This building was converted first to a Catholic church and then, in the early 1980s, to its current form as Mount Neboh Baptist Church. (See synagogues in the "Upper West Side" chapter for more information.)

Former First Hungarian Congregation Ohab Zedek (Religious Home of Cantor Rosenblatt)

18 West 116th Street (between Fifth and Sixth avenues)
Subway: 2 or 3 train to 116th Street

The First Hungarian Ohab Zedek congregation was founded on Norfolk Street on the Lower East Side in 1873. It moved around within the neighborhood, with stints at 70 Columbia Street and 172 Norfolk Street, the site of today's Angel Orensanz Center, which is the oldest surviving synagogue in New York and the fourth oldest in the United States.

In 1906, the congregation moved into Harlem, where many other synagogues had relocated to service the growing Jewish population. This site is most known for its association with Cantor Yossele Rosenblatt, who sang there (see below).

Two decades later, as Jews started moving out of Harlem and into the Upper West Side, the congregation relocated to 118 West Ninety-Fifth Street and remained Orthodox. The building on 116th Street was converted to a Baptist Temple Church, which occupied the location for many decades until it was demolished. Around 2008, the roof caved in, but the structure was saved. The sole remaining signs of its Jewish past are the Stars of David on both sides of the exterior. The building has been partly demolished and is currently vacant.

Background

Cantor Yossele Rosenblatt came from a family of cantors. He led a choir at a young age and published several songs as a teen. After serving as a cantor for this congregation, he toured to make more money. He famously turned down $1,000 per night, a great sum at the time, because it conflicted with his religious practices. He was later offered a part in the first talkie, *The Jazz Singer*, but declined to appear on screen for religious reasons. He did not think wearing makeup or singing live with women was compatible with his beliefs. The producers solved the problem by including scenes of Rosenblatt in concert. His techniques, such as his *krekhts*, or sobs, have been adopted by cantors globally. He would "deliberately allow his voice to crack to convey the emotion of what he was singing." He also invented ways for alleviating strained singing voices.[11]

Former Institutional Synagogue
112 West 116th Street
Subway: 2 or 3 train to 116th Street

Rabbi Herbert Goldstein formulated a new idea for an Orthodox shul. He envisioned a synagogue that would combine services similar to those offered in the three types of institutions already existing separately in Harlem, namely, the synagogue, the place of Jewish education, and the community center. His hope was to attract, engage, and retain new members.

The Institutional Synagogue was designed like a community center. It included not only a synagogue, but also a gym and swimming pool, and it was dubbed "shul with the pool." It introduced key synagogal features that are commonplace today, including sermons in English, cultural activities, and outreach programs.[12]

As the Jewish population in Harlem relocated to the Upper West Side, so did this congregation. In the 1920s, it moved to 122 West Seventy-Sixth Street, although it kept the Harlem location as a branch for two more decades. In the early 1940s, due to increasing financial problems and decreasing membership, the Harlem branch was eliminated. Currently, the building houses the Salvation and Deliverance Church. No trace of its synagogue past remains inside.

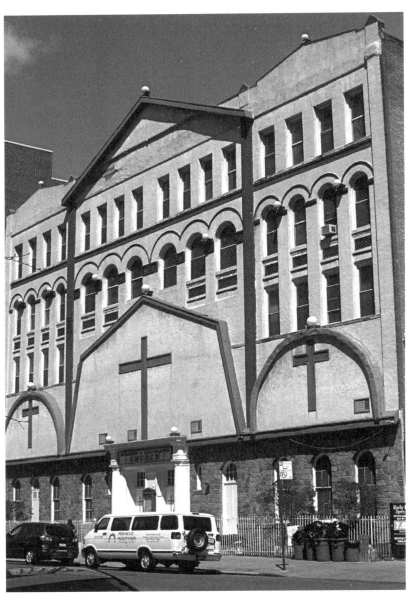

The site of the celebrated Institutional Synagogue, founded in 1917 by the maverick Rabbi Herbert Goldstein. It strove to combine religion and education in a YMCA-type setting. (Photograph by Jessica Siemens.)

Old Broadway Synagogue (Orthodox)
15 Old Broadway (half-block east of Broadway between 125th and 126th streets)
Telephone: (212) 662-9767
Web site: oldbroadwaysynagogue.blogspot.com
Subway: 1 train to 125th Street

There are few vestiges of Jewish life still operating in Jewish Harlem, but one is the Old Broadway Synagogue, off 125th Street. Incorporated in 1911 by immigrant Morris Schiff, the temple located to Harlem during its heyday of Jewish congregations. The synagogue's historical records show that congregants initially convened in storefronts and "purportedly in the back room of a bar until the Congregation purchased a house on Old Broadway."[13]

Former Temple Israel
201 Lenox Avenue (at 121st Street)
Subway: 2 or 3 train to 125th Street

As you walk past this building on a Sunday afternoon, you may hear lively music. Observe the building carefully and you will see details of its Jewish past in the architecture. You can see Stars of David at the top of the four enormous columns. Cross the street and look straight ahead through the stained-glass windows to see the very faded Star of David. Inside, you can see the old ark where the Torah was kept and Hebrew writings on the sacristy walls. The balcony where Orthodox Jewish women once sat during services remains.

Originally named Congregation Hand in Hand, the temple started in 1870 on 125th Street as Jews moved into Harlem. Congregants came from modest backgrounds. The temple's records state that its primarily German founders were "of moderate circumstances, many of them having small stores on Third Avenue and living behind their shops."

Four years later, the congregation moved to 124th Street. It relocated to East 116th Street two years later. In 1888, the congregation moved to the former site of the Holy Trinity Episcopal Church. It was common at the time for temples to acquire church buildings.

As the neighborhood boomed around 1910, the congregation sold its building for a large profit and moved to Lenox Avenue and 121st Street. Finally, thirteen years later, the congregation, like many others, relocated to the Upper West Side.

Today, the Lenox and 121st Street building houses Mt. Olivet Baptist Church. Temple Israel's congregation is now located at 112 East Seventy-Fifth Street.

For its part, the Mount Olivet Baptist Church is prominent in central Harlem, hosting speakers ranging from the late Venezuelan president Hugo Chavez to former American presidential candidate Howard Dean.

Eateries: Harlem

Harlem and Morningside Heights do not have any Jewish-style restaurants at present. For visitors interested in trying famous Harlem eateries that offer soul food, two of the most popular places are Sylvia's and Amy Ruth's.

Sylvia's
328 Lenox Avenue (between 126th and 127th streets)
Telephone: (212) 996-0660
Web site: www.sylviasrestaurant.com
Prices: Moderate
Subway: 2 or 3 train to 125th Street

The "Queen of Soul Food," Sylvia Woods was the creator and owner of the renowned Sylvia's Restaurant, located in Harlem since 1962. Sylvia's is a must-see for its legendary status. The restaurant exemplifies the Woods family's unlikely rise to prominence. It was also important as one of the few places that attracted tourists during Harlem's higher crime days of the 1970s and 1980s.

As you dine at Sylvia's, glance around the restaurant. Notice the pictures of its owners and celebrities who have visited this Harlem eating institution.

Background

Sylvia Woods was brought up in rural Hemingway, South Carolina. As an adult, she decided to "trade cotton fields for the bright lights of New York City." In 1944, she waitressed at Johnson's luncheonette. In 1962, fate would hand the budding entrepreneur an opportunity. Mr. Johnson agreed to sell her the luncheonette, which was a simple counter with a few booths. Sylvia financed the deal by borrowing from her mother, Julia Pressley, a farmer. Pressley put up her farm as collateral for the mortgage.[14]

Sylvia Woods died in 2012.

Amy Ruth's
113 West 116th Street (between Sixth and Seventh avenues)
Telephone: (212) 280-8779
Web site: www.amyruthsharlem.com
Prices: Moderate
Subway: 2 or 3 train to 116th Street

Established in 1998, Amy Ruth's is named after the owner's grandmother Amy Ruth Moore Bass and is famous for its authentic Southern cuisine. The restaurant is known for its waffles named after famous figures, such as the Reverend Al Sharpton (chicken and waffles).

Eateries: Morningside Heights

Community
2893 Broadway (between 112th and 113th streets)
Telephone: (212) 665-2800
Web site: www.communityrestaurant.com
Prices: Moderate
Subway: 1 train to 110th Street

Try the sausage and eggs with toast or the roasted chicken for two at this trendy, popular restaurant that specializes in brunch food with natural ingredients.

Kitchenette

1272 Amsterdam Avenue (between 122nd and 123rd streets)
Telephone: (212) 531-7600
Web site: www.kitchenetterestaurant.com
Prices: Moderate
Subway: 1 train to 125th Street

Try the South Ferry sandwich of roast turkey and jalapeno jack cheese or the barbeque turkey meatloaf sandwich. Ask about the blue plate specials, such as the taco pie or smothered fried chicken.

Le Monde Bistro

2885 Broadway (between 112th and 113th streets)
Telephone: (212) 531-3939
Web site: www.lemondenyc.com
Prices: Moderate
Subway: 1 train to 110th Street

Try the coq au vin at this French bistro located near Columbia University. Diners rave about the mussels. Ask about the daily special, ranging from roasted monkfish to sautéed lobster to short ribs in red wine.

Washington Heights

Explore the Jewish culture in the lesser-known Washington Heights area. Tour Yeshiva University and peruse its impressive archive. Visit historic synagogues such as Khal Adath Jeshurun (KAJ), with its unique German heritage. Explore this ever-changing neighborhood and the role that refusniks (Jews trying to leave the Soviet Union) have played in it. And take in the distinctive natural landscapes, Fort Tryon Park, and scenic views of the city.

History of Jewish Washington Heights

Significant Jewish settlement in Washington Heights began with Yeshiva University (YU). Though founded downtown, the university relocated uptown in the mid-1920s. The faculty followed it, thereby establishing a small but prominent Jewish community. German Jews also came to this area both before and after the Holocaust. All of this coalesced when noted rabbi Joseph Breuer arrived from Germany in the 1930s. The Jews who identified with the teachings of his grandfather, Samson Hirsch, begged him to become their leader. He accepted and started what is now Congregation Khal Adath Jeshurun (see section below on historic synagogues), also known as KAJ.

German Jews continued to move to Washington Heights primarily because their countrymen were already living there and they shared a common language. The Jewish population increased from 1933 to 1942 as many fled Nazi Germany.

Later arrivals were not always of German descent but were interested in the Orthodox community established by Breuer and others. The community continued to flourish until the 1980s, when people moved to the suburbs. Unlike in other areas,

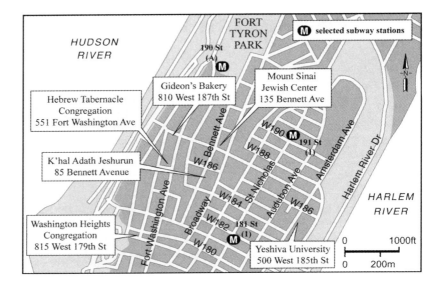

efforts were made to sustain the size of the Jewish community
here by embarking on a full-scale resettlement program for newly
emigrating Russian Jews. Since then, the community has thrived.
Further strengthening the neighborhood are the many young
Orthodox families who have been priced out of the Upper West
Side and have decided to settle in Washington Heights.

One of the most significant Jewish sites in Washington Heights
is Yeshiva University.

Places of Interest

Yeshiva University
500 West 185th Street (at Amsterdam Avenue)
Telephone: (212) 960-5400
Web site: www.yu.edu
Subway: 1 or A train to 181st Street

Amidst the Jewish and Latino cultures in the diverse neighborhood of
Washington Heights stands the oldest university in the United States
that combines Jewish scholarship with secular subjects, Yeshiva

University. It had its origins in 1886 on the bustling Lower East Side
as part of the yeshiva Etz Chaim. In March 1928, the Yeshiva College
formed after Etz Chaim merged with the Rabbi Isaac Elchanan
Theological Seminary. The campus in Washington Heights was born.[1]

Walk over to David H. Zysman Hall and observe its charming
Moorish architecture. If possible, view the ornate auditorium
inside that hosts key YU events. The best way to see this is
through a public program or a campus tour.

Background

In 1932, during the Great Depression, the university's first
commencement honored nineteen graduates. Probably the two
most famous women to receive honorary degrees were Eleanor
Roosevelt in 1952 and Golda Meir in 1973. In 1954, Stern College, a
liberal-arts school for women, opened at 33rd Street and Lexington
Avenue. (See Greenwich Village and East Village chapter.)

Today, Yeshiva University runs four campuses: the main one
described here that caters to male undergraduates and a variety of
graduate students; the Beren Campus, which includes Stern College
for female students; the Resnick Campus in the Bronx that includes
the famed Albert Einstein College of Medicine; and the Brookdale
Center in Greenwich Village that serves as a law school.[2]

One of YU's lesser-known but unique programs is Yemenite
studies. The Yemenite Institute opened in 1986, offering courses
in Yemenite history, culture, and tradition.

If you are interested in scholarship or archives, pay a visit to
the university's special collections library. Make an appointment
at archives@yu.edu.[3]

Peruse the collections of rare books and archival records, many
of which are in Hebrew. Also visit the Sephardic reference section
for materials in Ladino (Judeo-Spanish).[4] Perhaps the most famous
item in the collections is the elaborately illustrated Prague Bible
of 1488, by the scribe Mattathias ben Jonah of Laun, Bohemia.[5]

"Moscow on the Hudson" Neighborhood

On the corner of 184th Street and Bennett Avenue, you will
see a street sign for Pierto Pincassa Plaza. This area embodies the
struggles of Soviet Jewry. Pierto Pincassa was a refusnik. At the

time, it was illegal to practice Judaism in the USSR but also illegal to leave the country. Many Soviet Jews experienced this plight.

Jacob Birnbaum, a student at Yeshiva University and resident of Washington Heights, spearheaded a movement to help Soviet Jews find freedom, Student Struggle for Soviet Jewry. He held rallies in front of Soviet missions. His efforts caught on and eventually won the attention of federal officials, who helped resettle refusniks.

During the neighborhood's decline in the 1970s and 1980s, many older Jews remained, and area activists facilitated the arrival of Soviet Union refusniks. Laurie Tobias Cohen, executive director of the Lower East Side Jewish Conservancy, explains this development. "This neighborhood became a home to thousands of Soviet Jews. Many refusniks, rather than settling in Israel, chose to come to the United States." With this in mind, a consortium of many social nonprofits formed the Jewish Community Council of Washington Heights, and a full-fledged program of resettlement was born. Cohen recalls, "The fabric of the neighborhood changed. The point is that the vision for this resettlement served as a bridge during this period of decline. After this period, gentrification occurred." The neighborhood is now populated by many younger Orthodox Jews.

Historic Synagogues

Hebrew Tabernacle of Washington Heights (Reform)
551 Fort Washington Avenue (at 185th Street)
Telephone: (212) 568-8304
Web site: www.hebrewtabernacle.org
Subway: A train to 181st Street

Reverend Lissman and Adolph Schwarzbaum founded the temple in 1906 at 218 West 130th Street in Harlem, in response to the lack of education for Jewish youth. "From its inception the mode of service has been a mixture of Conservative and Reform traditions," notes the congregation-produced book *The History of Hebrew Tabernacle*. "Wearing head coverings and *tallis* during services followed the conservative custom; the mixed choir and especially the use of an organ, on the other hand, had been among the most fought over issues in the nineteenth century debate regarding synagogue reforms in Germany." Later, the congregation moved to its present location in Washington Heights.

For more of the history of this temple, download *The History of Hebrew Tabernacle* from their web site, www.hebrewtabernacle.org.

Khal Adath Jeshurun (Orthodox)
85 Bennett Avenue
Telephone: (212) 923-3582
Web site: www.kajinc.org
Subway: A train to 181st Street

This synagogue traces its roots to a prewar Jewish community led by the famed Samson Raphael Hirsch, who rejected the Reform-dominated politics and religious life of mid-nineteenth-century Frankfurt, Germany. Today, Khal Adath Jeshurun is based on Hirsch's philosophy of *torah im derech eretz* ("the way of the land") from the mid-nineteenth century.

Rabbi Joseph Breuer, Hirsch's grandson, founded the congregation. Breuer arrived in New York in 1939 and was asked to lead a small congregation. It later blossomed into a large congregation that would stand for its German ancestors' values—a "bastion of Independent Orthodoxy."

The growing congregation moved to several locations for more room and, in one case, because of a fire. The current shul was built in 1952 and extensively renovated in 2001.

Fulfilling the founders' vision of a "full-service community," KAJ offers not only a synagogue, but also schools, a yeshiva, social halls, and mikvah. The members of the congregation still practice uniquely German rituals. Avram Guttman, the grandson of the founder and a member of the board of trustees, notes the style of daven or prayer, the unique music, and the participation of the choir as distinctive features. "The text of our davening follows the general German custom with certain specific exceptions which follow the customs of the Frankfurt community which were accepted here," he comments. "We also insert the Piyutim on special Shabbosos and on Yom Tov which many other congregations no longer say."

Visual customs include the beautiful floral decorations, the three white poroches (curtains that cover the door to the ark housing the Torah scrolls), the white seat covers, and the white carpeting that gives the shul a special feeling between Rosh Hashanah and Yom Kippur. On Chanukah there is a special candle lighting on each of the eight nights, in which the chazzan ascends steps to light an eight-foot-high menorah with specially made long candles.

Washington Heights Congregation ("The Bridge Shul") (Orthodox)
135 Bennett Avenue
Telephone: (212) 923-4407
Web site: www.bridgeshul.com
Subway: A train to 181st Street

This shul was founded in 1905 on 161st Street. For many years it was the sole Orthodox congregation in this part of Washington Heights. It opened a Talmud Torah (a school teaching various Jewish subjects) with a sizable student body. Soon afterward, the congregation expanded to a second building.[6]

During the late 1960s and the 1970s, the congregation lost steam. Many congregants moved elsewhere as the neighborhood's safety and desirability diminished. In 1971 the shul, under "dynamic new leadership," relocated to 179th Street, where it would remain for forty-three years. In May 2014, the Bridge Shul moved again, to a smaller, less costly space at 135 Bennett Avenue (corner of 187th Street) on the lower level of Mount Sinai Jewish Center.

Eateries

Chop Chop (Kosher)
501 West 184th Street (between Amsterdam and Audubon avenues)
Telephone: (212) 246-7246
Web site: www.chopchopkosher.com
Prices: Moderate
Subway: A train to 181st Street

The menu lists Chinese food and sushi, such as wonton soup, egg rolls, lemon chicken, and sashimi.

Gideon's Bakery (Kosher)
810 West 187th Street
Telephone: (212) 927-9262
Prices: Inexpensive
Subway: A train to 181st Street

Tucked away in the upper corner of Washington Heights, this low-profile kosher bakery is known for its Hungarian rye and raisin pumpernickel and hamantaschen. It serves sandwiches during the week.

Golan Heights (Kosher)
2553 Amsterdam Avenue (between 186th and 187th streets)
Telephone: (212) 795-7842
Prices: Inexpensive
Subway: 1 train to 181st Street

Frequented by Yeshiva University students, Golan Heights provides inexpensive fare such as falafel, shawarma, and schnitzel. Locals recommend that if ordering anything on pita bread, a diner should request it with hummus and chips.

Q'Kachapa
1552 St. Nicholas Avenue (at 187th Street)
Telephone: (212) 928-2898
Prices: Moderate
Subway: 1 or A train to 181st Street

If you are looking for Latin American food in this neighborhood, try Q'Kachapa. Diners rave about the sweet plantains, Venezuelan-style burritos, and arepas.

Suggested Tour Routes

Lower Manhattan/Downtown/Tribeca

Time: One to two days, depending if the Statue of Liberty and
Ellis Island are included

Start at the Staten Island Ferry at South Ferry (subway: 1
train) and observe the Monument to the Immigrants. Walk up
State Street to Castle Gardens. Next to Castle Gardens, observe
the plaque to Emma Lazarus. Purchase tickets to the Statue of
Liberty and Ellis Island. Board the ferry at this location, which
takes you to both destinations.

The ferry returning from Ellis Island will leave you at Battery
Park. Go north on State Street and make a left on Battery Place.
Follow Battery Place to the Museum of Jewish Heritage. Follow
the route back by walking south on Battery Place, which turns into
State Street. Make a left on Pearl Street and a left on Broad Street
to Fraunces Tavern, to visit the museum or the historic tavern or
both. Make a right on South William Street to see the site of the
original synagogue in New York City (today a parking garage).
Cut across Stone Street to Mill Street and enjoy Revolutionary-
themed eateries and bars.

Lower East Side

Time: Two to three days

The Lower East Side is replete with Jewish sites. You may wish to
join a tour of them at the Lower East Side Jewish Conservancy.

217

Theme: Immigrant Life and Food

Start off at the Museum at Eldridge Street, between Canal and Division. View the impressive sanctuary and choose between several tours. Continue to the Tenement Museum on Orchard Street by walking north to Delancey Street and making a right. Go three blocks to Orchard Street. Choose one or two tours of the tenements. Consider also one of the neighborhood tours, or ask about the special food tour. Make sure to call ahead for reservations.

Walk north on Orchard Street to Houston. Make a right and proceed to the corner of Ludlow Street to have lunch at Katz's Deli. Remember to hold on to the ticket given to you at the entrance. From Katz's, make a left and visit Russ and Daughters, where you can shop for smoked fish, chocolates, and other delicacies. Continue west on Houston for two blocks to Yonah Shimmel Knish Bakery and choose a flavor to try. Turn back on Houston and walk a few blocks east to Essex Street. Make a right and head past Rivington. Browse the many shops at Essex Street Market. Exiting the market, go back to Rivington. Make a right and continue to Suffolk. Visit the Streit's Matzo Factory. See if you can catch a behind-the-scenes tour of matzo making.

Walk back to Essex and continue south to Grand Street, where you can try a pickle at the Pickle Guys. Continue south to Hester Street. Browse the shops in what was once the heart of Jewish immigrant life. Walk back to Grand and make a right, heading east to Clinton Street. Stop in Kossar's Bialys and the Doughnut Plant. On the north side of the street one block up, visit the Lower East Side Jewish Conservancy's Visitor Center. Walk one block south to East Broadway, where you'll pass the former Shtiebel Row and see the one-room synagogues. Nearby, view the *Forward* Building and the opposing Jarmulowsky's Bank Building. Notice the site of the former Garden Cafeteria at 165 East Broadway. Learn the remarkable stories of these buildings in the Lower East Side chapter of this book. Walk east to 228 East Broadway and notice the art-deco décor on the front of the former Bialystoker Home for the Aged building. Walk around the eastern side and admire the colorful mural.

Continue west on East Broadway and notice the Amalgamated Dwellings and Educational Alliance buildings at 197 East Broadway, between Clinton and Suffolk. Walk farther west and visit Nathan Strauss Square, the small plot at the intersection of East Broadway, Essex, Canal, and Rutgers streets. At Canal and East Broadway, observe the once ornate but now hidden Loew's Canal Street Theater above the storefront. For place to rest, visit the Seward Park Branch of the New York Public Library at 192 East Broadway and Jefferson streets, an important library of material on immigrants' lives. Walk south to Henry Street, and at 263–265, view the famed Henry Street Settlement. See if there are any programs or volunteer opportunities of interest to you. If you want to catch a show in a historically significant building, head back north to the Harry De Jur Playhouse of Henry Street Settlement, at 466 Grand Street.

Theme: Historic Synagogues

Start at the Angel Orensanz Foundation Center for the Arts at 172 Norfolk Street by taking the J, M, or Z train to Essex Street. From the subway, head north for two blocks on Essex, make a right on Stanton, and then a left on Norfolk. Walk to Houston and make a right, then go to Clinton and make another right. View Congregation Chasam Sopher at 8 Clinton Street and continue to the Stanton Shul at 180 Stanton Street. View the exterior, or make an appointment (or attend a service) to view the unique interior. Then walk several blocks south to Broome Street and turn right. Walk west to Allen Street and view the Greek congregation Kehila Kedosha Janina (Holy Community of Janina) at 280 Broom Street. Then walk back east to Grand Street to Beth Hamedrash Hagadol. View this synagogue only from the outside, since you cannot enter the deteriorating building. Make a left on Grand and continue several blocks to the Bialystoker Synagogue, at 7 Bialystoker Place. Schedule an appointment in order to visit the interior.

Greenwich Village/East Village, Chelsea, and Midtown

Time: Two to three days, depending on time spent at Center for
   Jewish History

Day One

Start your visit in the former Jewish Rialto, the Yiddish theater
district on Second Avenue and Houston Street. The following sites
can be found on Second Avenue: former Yiddish theaters such as
the Orpheum at St. Mark's Place (currently a modern theater
showing off-Broadway productions like *Stomp*); the former
Commodore Theater on Sixth Street, which is now the Emigrant
Bank (break for a pastry at the neighborhood staple Moishe's
Bakery at Seventh Street); and the former Yiddish Art Theater on
Twelfth Street, now known as the Village East Cinemas. Observe
the faded, historic Yiddish Walk of Fame on the eastern side of
Second Avenue between Tenth and Eleventh streets. At Tenth,
make a right and walk two blocks to the Russian Baths between
First Avenue and Avenue A, where you can get a massage or sweat
in any of the many saunas.

Head four blocks south and one block west to the Sixth Street
Community Synagogue, the site of the German Lutheran church
whose congregation perished in the *General Slocum* disaster
of 1904. Check listings for klezmer concerts at the synagogue.
Walk down to Fourth Street and make a right, crossing Second
Avenue and the Bowery to Lafayette to reach the former Hebrew
Immigrant Aid Society Building (now the Joseph Papp Public
Theater). Read the history of the building and check listings of
performances. Continue on Fourth Street, heading west between
Broadway and Mercer to Hebrew Union College. View the exhibit
on the ground floor. Continue west one block to Greene Street and
make a right to Washington Place to see the site of the Triangle
Shirtwaist Factory fire.

For lunch, consider Veselka's at Second Avenue and Ninth
Street.

Day Two (and day three, if spending most of day two at the Center for Jewish History)

Walk west on Eleventh Street and view one of Shearith Israel's cemeteries between Fifth and Sixth avenues. Go north five blocks to the world-renowned Center for Jewish History, at 15 West Sixteenth Street between Fifth and Sixth avenues. Spend the bulk of the afternoon here visiting the many exhibits and archives. See if you can catch a tour or browse the American Jewish Historical Society (AJHS), the American Sephardi Federation (ASF), the Yeshiva University Museum (YU Museum), or the YIVO Institute for Jewish Research (YIVO).

Walk to Seventh Avenue and take the 1, 2, or 3 train uptown to Thirty-Fourth Street. Exit the station and see Macy's flagship store. Learn about its little-known Jewish history. Shop in the store or look at the famed window displays. Then walk to Thirty-Ninth Street to view the Garment Center Monument. Walk up to Forty-Seventh Street, make a right, and walk one block to Sixth Avenue. You are in the famed Diamond District. Browse the stores and witness the frenzied dealings (weekdays only). If you want to see more Jewish archives, continue east to Fifth Avenue and walk a few blocks south to Forty-Second Street. Enter the famed New York Public Library and visit the exhibits and collections in the Jewish Division.

If you have a craving for deli food, walk toward uptown for seven blocks and order a sandwich at the iconic Carnegie Deli on Seventh Avenue between Fifty-Fourth and Fifty-Fifth streets. If you want to hear a world-class concert, head two blocks up to Fifty-Seventh Street and Seventh Avenue to the historic Carnegie Hall and check performance listings. See if you can catch a backstage tour.

If you have the energy, walk east several blocks to Lexington Avenue and Fifty-Fifth Street to view the historic Central Synagogue.

Upper East Side and Upper West Side

Time: One day (two if visiting the Jewish Museum)

Start at the magnificent Temple Emanu-El at Sixty-Fifth Street
and Fifth Avenue. Visit the museum and try to view the grandiose
sanctuary. Walk to Lexington Avenue and up to Sixty-Eighth
Street for the subway. Take the 6 train uptown to Ninety-Sixth
Street. Exit the station and walk south for four blocks to Ninety-
Second Street. Visit the best Young Men's Hebrew Association
(YMHA) in the nation and see if any of the lectures, concerts, or
workshops interest you. Walk three blocks west to Fifth Avenue
and spend a couple of hours at the Jewish Museum.

Walk downtown to Eighty-Sixth Street. Take the M86 bus west
to Amsterdam. Try the delicacies at Barney Greengrass. Walk
two blocks west to West End Avenue and two blocks north to
Eighty-Eighth Street, to the historic B'nai Jeshurun. Walk back
to Broadway and make a right. Go down eight blocks and shop
at the local-favorite market, Zabar's. Take the number 1 train
at Seventy-Ninth Street downtown to Sixty-Sixth Street. See if
you can catch a tour at the monumental Lincoln Center for the
Performing Arts. Check listings for concerts, dances, or operas,
or just marvel at the murals. Walk four blocks up to Seventieth
Street and east three blocks to Central Park West to the oldest
Ashkenazic congregation in North America, Shearith Israel (also
called the Spanish and Portuguese Synagogue).

Harlem and Morningside Heights

Time: One day

Start your trip by taking the A, B, C, or D train to 125th Street.
View the former site of Blumstein's (currently part of Touro
College), one of the most famous department stores in the area
for many decades. Walk a few blocks east to the Lenox Lounge
and check listings for live music. Head south five blocks to 120th
Street and look at the former residences of Gertrude Edelstein

(Molly Goldberg), Lena Himmelstein, and Richard Rodgers. Walk one block north to Lenox Avenue and 121st Street and view the former Congregation Chebra Ukadisha B'nai Mikalwarie (currently Ebenezer Gospel Tabernacle). Continue viewing former famous synagogues by heading south to 116th Street and Fifth Avenue, to the First Hungarian Congregation Ohab Zedek, the religious home of Cantor Rosenblatt. Walk past the nearby former Institutional Synagogue (currently Salvation and Deliverance Church). For lunch, try Amy Ruth's for soul food at 116th Street, one block west between Sixth and Seventh avenues. If you are interested in seeing the premier Conservative Jewish seminary, walk up to 123rd Street and then go west for five blocks to reach the Jewish Theological Seminary. Ask if you can visit the library or take a campus tour.

Washington Heights

Time: One-half to a whole day

Start at Yeshiva University at West 185th Street and Amsterdam by taking the 1 or A train to 181st Street. Catch a campus tour and see if you can visit the main building, Zysman Hall. Visit the library and, if you are interested in archives, make an appointment to view the special collections, which include the rare books and Sephardic reference room. Explore the neighborhood around Yeshiva University. Walk to 184th Street and east to Bennett Avenue to view the sign for Pierto Pincassa Plaza that remains from the 1980s. Read the background on the area's struggle to help Soviet Jewry. Nearby on Bennett Avenue is the German congregation Khal Adath Jeshurun. If it is open, view the sanctuary or join a service. Walk up to 187th Street and go west a few avenues, past Fort Washington Avenue, to try a treat at Gideon's Bakery.

Notes

Introduction

1. Gomez Mill House archives and history, www.gomez.org/archivedsite/articles02.html.

2. Ibid.

3. Quotes by New Amsterdammers, www.fulkerson.org/1-quotes.html.

4. Jeffrey Gurock, *Orthodox Jews in America* (Bloomington: Indiana University Press, 2009).

5. Jewish Virtual Library, www.jewishvirtuallibrary.org.

6. Gurock.

7. "Yearbook of Immigration Statistics: 2009—Supplemental Table 2," accessed April 30, 2010.

8. Jewish Virtual Library.

9. Ronald Sanders, *The Lower East Side Jews: An Immigrant Generation* (New York: Dover, 1987), 51.

10. www.pbs.org.

11. "The Jewish Community Study of New York: 2011," *United Jewish Appeal*, www.ujafedny.org/jewish-community-study-fast-facts/.

Lower Manhattan

1. National Park Service, www.nps.gov.

2. Ibid.

3. Ibid.

4. www.frauncestavern.com/room-dinglewhiskeybar.php.

5. Museum of Jewish Heritage annual reports.

6. Museum of Jewish Heritage, www.mjhnyc.org.

7. Ibid.

8. Jake Rajs, *New York City Landmarks* (New York: Antique Collectors' Club, 2012), 24.

9. Ibid., 16.

10. Ellis Island timeline, Ellis Island Foundation (2000).

11. Rajs, 22.

12. Ellis Island Museum, www.ellisisland.org/genealogy.

13. Ibid.

14. www.nyc-architecture.com; American Jewish Historical Society, www.ajhs.org.

15. The Foundation for the Advancement of Sephardic Studies and Culture, www.sephardicstudies.org/judah.html, © 1967–2004.

16. Ibid.

17. Ibid.

18. Ibid

19. Ibid.

20. Ibid.

21. International working party for the documentation and conservation of buildings, sites, and neighborhoods of the modern movement, http://docomomo-us.org/register/fiche/civic_center_synagogue.

22. Kutsher's Tribeca, http://kutsherstribeca.com/about/.

Lower East Side

1. Tenement Museum publicity materials and Web site, www.tenement.org.

2. Ibid.

3. "Eddie Cantor Dead," *New York Times*, October 11, 1964.

4. "Dedication of a New Building for the Institute," *New York Times*, November 9, 1891.

5. Joyce Mendelsohn, *Lower East Side: Remembered and Revisited* (New York: Columbia University Press, 2009), 206.

6. www.essexstreetmarket.com/history.html.

7. www.placematters.net/node/1205.

8. Hebrew Free Loan Society, www.hfls.org/about-us/history.

9. Lawrence Epstein, *At the Edge of a Dream: The Story of Jewish Immigrants on New York's Lower East Side* (New York: Wiley, 2007).

10. David Carson Berry, "Gambling with Chromaticism? Extra-Diatonic Melodic Expression in the Songs of Irving Berlin," *Theory and Practice* 26 (2001): 21–85.

11. "Banker's Hasty Departure," *New York Times*, September 27, 1914.

12. Mendelsohn, 59.

13. Ibid., 139.

14. "Chinatown Treasure: Long Lost Theater Rediscovered," *New York Post*, January 10, 2010.

15. Ibid.

16. Lower East Side Jewish Conservancy publicity materials and Web site, www.lesjc.org/about-LESJC.htm.

17. Mendelsohn, 94–95.

18. Ibid.

19. Ibid., 67.

20. Barry Feldman (New York City tour guide), interview with author, April 2012.

21. New York City Department of Parks and Recreation Web site, accessed February 17, 2011.

22. Mendelsohn, 191–93.

23. "Ratner's Closes, for the Last Time," www.LowerManhattan. Info., December 16, 2004; accessed August 25, 2006.

24. www.nytimes.com/2011/04/10/realestate/10streetscapes. html.

25. Ibid.

26. "Playgrounds and Public Recreation (1898–1929)," New York City Department of Parks and Recreation Web site, accessed July 24, 2011.

27. Mendelsohn, 209.

28. Ibid., 210.

29. Ibid.

30. www.ujces.org/mission.htm.

31. Mendelsohn, 176.

32. Ibid., 148.

33. Ibid., 119.

34. Ibid.

35. Ibid.

36. www.neighborhoodpreservationcenter.org/db/bb_files/87-ANSHE-SLONIM.pdf, accessed October 12, 2011.

37. Mendelsohn, 227.

38. Ibid.

39. Al Orensanz, "From Anshe Chesed to Angel Orensanz: 156 Years at 172 Norfolk Street," www.orensanz.org/pdf/orensanz-booklet.pdf.

40. Gerard Wolfe, *The Synagogues of New York's Lower East*

Side (New York: Fordham University Press, 2013), 99.

41. Ibid., 100.

42. Jeffrey S. Gurock, *The History of Judaism in America: Transplantations, Transformations, and Reconciliations,* vol. 5, *American Jewish History* (Abingdon, UK: Taylor & Francis, 1998).

43. Wolfe, 41.

44. Mendelsohn, 220.

45. Wolfe, 44.

46. Ibid.

47. Mendelsohn, 111.

48. Wolfe, 105.

49. Thomas Lueck, "Questions Rise from the Dust of an Old Synagogue," *New York Times*, March 2006.

50. Mendelsohn, 156.

51. www.doughnutplant.com.

52. www.economycandy.com.

53. Rajs, 67.

54. Mendelsohn, 113.

55. www.pickleguys.com.

56.   www.npr.org/templates/transcript/transcript.php?storyId=173264635.

57. "The Lower East Side Traditions and Transitions," *The Villager*, October 17, 2007, www.thevillager.com/villager_233/bakerystilldishing.html.

58. www.cityroom.blog.nytimes.com.

59. Eric Asimov, "$25 and Under," *New York Times*, December 27, 1996, www.nytimes.com, accessed June 21, 2007.

Greenwich Village and East Village

1. Judith Thissen, "Reconsidering the Decline of the New York Yiddish Theatre in the Early 1900s" (Theatre Survey 44:2,2003).

2. Ibid.

3. www.villageeastcinema.com/angelika_history.asp.

4. Ibid.

5. http://travel.nytimes.com/2007/01/26/travel.

6. Greenwich Village Society for Historic Preservation, www.gvshp.org/blog/2011/03/01/cafe-royal/.

7. www.nationalyiddishtheatre.org/about.html.

8. Richard Simonson, "Where Have You Gone, Molly Picon," *New York Times*, March 19, 2006.

9. S. M. Melamed, "The Yiddish Stage," *New York Times*, September 27, 1925.

10. www.cinematreasures.org/theaters/22028.

11. Ibid.

12. www.hias.org.

13. Leon Stein, *The Triangle Fire* (Ithaca: Cornell University Press, 1962).

14. Stein.

Chelsea and Midtown

1. www.cjh.org.

2. Ibid.

3. Ibid.

4. Carnegie Hall library and Web site.

5. Ibid.

6. Ibid.

7. Ibid.

8. Kenneth T. Jackson, ed., *The Encyclopedia of New York City* (New Haven: New York Historical Society/Yale University Press, 1995), 332.

9. Jane Hanson, *Jane's New York*, WNBC-TV.

10. Ibid.

11. Elaine S. Abelson, "R. H. Macy," in *The Encyclopedia of New York City*, ed. Kenneth T. Jackson, 2nd ed. (New Haven: Yale University Press, 2010), 1102.

12. Dorot Jewish Division, New York Public Library publicity materials and Web site.

13. Ibid.

14. Ibid.

15. Ibid.

16. Stern College for Women at Yeshiva University publicity materials and Web site.

17. www.circle.org.

18. www.theactorstemple.org.

19. Ibid.

20. "Once a Realm of Stars, Temple is Now Bereft of Them, and Their Money," *New York Times*, November 18, 2011.

21. Ibid.

22. Christopher Gray, *New York Streetscapes* (New York: Harry N. Abrams, 2003), 188.

23. Ibid.

24. www.carnegiedeli.com.

25. www.2ndavedeli.com.

Upper East Side

1. Rajs, 194.

2. www.jewishmuseum.org.

3. www.mountsinai.org/about-us/who-we-are/history.

4. www.92y.org.

5. Ibid.

6. www.emanuelnyc.org.

7. Ibid.

8. "Madoff's Clients," *New York Times*, January 22, 2009.

9. Karen Zraick, "Four-alarm fire ravages Manhattan synagogue," Associated Press, July 11, 2011.

10. "The Edmond J. Safra Synagogue in New York City Is Inaugurated," *Yeshiva University News*, October 1, 2003.

Upper West Side

1. www.lincolncenter.org.

2. Donal Henahan, "Leonard Bernstein, 72, Music's Monarch, Dies," *New York Times*, October 15, 1990.

3. Jackie Wullschlager, *Chagall: A Biography* (New York: Knopf, 2008).

4. www.lincolncenter.org.

5. Ibid

6. Ibid.

7. www.jccmanhattan.org.

8. Ibid.

9. "Murray Klein, Who Helped Build Zabar's into Food Destination, Dies at 84," *New York Times*

10. Ibid.

11. www.bj.org.

12. www.jewishcenter.org/content.php?pg=vision&ID=243.

13. www.romemu.org.

14. www.shearithisrael.org.

15. Artie's Delicatessen publicity materials and Web site, www.arties83rd.net.

Harlem and Morningside Heights

1. www.flickr.com/photos/wallyg/1023834906/.

2. Ibid.

3. www.lenoxlounge.com/history.

4. "Lenox Lounge: A Harlem Night Spot," *New York Times*, January 10, 2013.

5. www.jewishvirtuallibrary.org/jsource/biography/Bryant.html.

6. www.rnh.com/bio/175/Rodgers-Richard.

7. www.jtsa.edu.

8. Ibid.

9. "What Distinguishes the UTJ from the Conservative Movement?", Union for Traditional Judaism, www.utj.org/faq#q7.

10. www/query.nytimes.com/gst/abstract.

11. West Side Institutional Synagogue, www.wsisny.org/wsis-history.html.

12. "National Register Information System," National Register of Historic Places. National Park Service, March 13, 2009.

13. New York City Chapter of American Guild of Organists, www.nycago.org/Organs/NYC/html/TempleIsrael.html.

14. www.sylviasrestaurant.com/about_us3.html.

Washington Heights

1. Yeshiva University museums publicity materials and Web site, www.yu.edu/libraries.

2. Ibid.

3. Ibid.

4. Ibid.

5. Ibid.

6. www.bridgeshul.com.

References

Books

The Encyclopedia of New York City. New Haven: New York Historical Society/Yale University Press, 1995.

Epstein, Lawerence. *At the Edge of a Dream*. New York: John Wiley and Sons, 2007.

Fertitta, Naomi. *New York: The Big City and Its Little Neighborhoods*. Universe, 2009.

Gurock, Jeffrey S. *The History of Judaism in America: Transplantations, Transformations, and Reconciliations*. In *American Jewish History*, Vol. 5. 1998.

———. *Orthodox Jews in America*. Bloomington: Indiana University Press, 2009.

Homberger, Eric. *The Historical Atlas of New York City*. New York: Henry Holt, 2005.

Markel, Howard. *Quarantine: East European Jewish Immigrants and New York City Epidemics of 1892*. Baltimore: Johns Hopkins University Press, 1997.

Mendelshohn, Joyce. *The Lower East Side Remembered and Revisited: A History and Guide to a Legendary New York Neighborhood*. New York: Columbia University Press, 2009.

Rajs, Jake. *New York City Landmarks*. New York: Antique Collectors Club, 2012.

Sanders, Ronald. *The Lower East Side: A Guide to Its Jewish Past in 99 New Photographs*. New York: Dover, 1980.

———. *The Lower East Side Jews: An Immigrant Generation*. New York: Dover, 1999.

Wolfe, Gerard. *The Synagogues of New York's Lower East Side*. New York: Fordham University Press, 2013.

Wolfman, Ira. *Jewish New York—Notable Neighborhoods and Memorable Moments*. New York: Universe, 2003.

Online Sources

Center for Jewish History (cjh. org)

Cinematreasures.org

Ellisisland.org

Frauncestavern.com

Gomez.org

istock.com

Jewfaq.org

jewishvirtuallibrary.org

Maggieblanck.com

Museum of Jewish Heritage (Mjhnyc.org)

Nationalyiddishtheatre.org

New York City municipal archives (nyc.gov/records)

NewYorkTimes.com archives

NPR.org

NYC-architecture.com

Orsenz.org

Sephardicstudies.org

Tenement.org

TheVillager.org

Wikipedia.com

Workman's Circle (Circle.org)

Yelp.com

Zagat.com

The author also consulted many museums', organizations', and restaurants' Web sites, as cited in the notes.

Interview Subjects

Laurie Tobias Cohen, Lower East Side Jewish Conservancy

Bonnie Dimun, Museum at Eldridge Street

Barry Feldman, Lower East Side Jewish Conservancy

Justin Ferate, Tours of the City

Avram Gutmann, KAJ Temple

Joyce Mendelsohn, author of *The Lower East Side Remembered and Revisited*

Martin Shore, Lower East Side Jewish Conservancy

Bryna Wasserman and Zalmen Mlotek, National Yiddish Theatre

Index